UNPUBLISHED Bo-FRAGMENTS IN TRANSLITERATION I (Bo 9536 – Bo 9736)

UNPUBLISHED Bo-FRAGMENTS IN TRANSLITERATION I
(Bo 9536 – Bo 9736)

OĞUZ SOYSAL

CHICAGO HITTITE DICTIONARY SUPPLEMENTS • 2
THE ORIENTAL INSTITUTE OF THE UNIVERSITY OF CHICAGO
CHICAGO • ILLINOIS

Library of Congress Control Number: 2015936211
ISBN-13: 978-1-61491-028-2

The Oriental Institute, Chicago

© 2015 by The University of Chicago. All rights reserved.
Published 2015. Printed in the United States of America.

THE ORIENTAL INSTITUTE OF THE UNIVERSITY OF CHICAGO
CHICAGO HITTITE DICTIONARY SUPPLEMENTS
NUMBER 2

Series Editors

Leslie Schramer

and

Thomas G. Urban

with the assistance of

Rebecca Cain

Cover Illustration

Middle Hittite anonymous royal prayer to the Sun-god (KUB 36.75 + Bo 9628 + Bo 9659 +)

Printed by Thomson-Shore, Dexter, Michigan USA

The paper used in this publication meets the minimum requirements of American National Standard for Information Services — Permanence of Paper for Printed Library Materials, ANSI Z39.48-1984.

∞

In Memoriam

Talât Sait Halman

(1931–2014)

TABLE OF CONTENTS

FOREWORD

This study is similar to *Ankara Arkeoloji Müzesinde Bulunan Boğazköy Tabletleri II / Boğazköy Tablets in the Archaeological Museum of Ankara II*, which was also dedicated to small Hittite fragments. After my long-term cooperation with Rukiye Akdoğan was completed and resulted in the cuneiform publication mentioned above by the Oriental Institute (CHDS 1) in 2011, I started another project involving the unpublished Hittite texts deposited in the Museum of Ancient Anatolian Civilizations in Ankara, the results of which are presented here.

Shortly before the publication of the cuneiform edition *Keilschrifturkunden aus Boghazköi* 60 (1990), the final volume of this series, all Boğazköy tablets — both published or unpublished — bearing the siglum "Bo" were transferred from the Staatliches Museum in Berlin to the Museum of Ancient Anatolian Civilizations in Ankara in 1987. The unpublished tablets which were returned to Turkey from Berlin were to be copied, studied, and published by a team of Turkish Hittitologists under the direction of Sedat Alp. The assignment of the fragments in question among the team members was considered as follows:

Bo 0008 – Bo 5717	Sedat Alp / Gül Ün
Bo 5719 – Bo 6086	Aygül Süel
Bo 6087 – Bo 6434	Ahmet Ünal
Bo 6435 – Bo 6842	Cem Karasu
Bo 6843 – Bo 7196	Belkıs Dinçol
Bo 7197 – Bo 7508	Hayri Ertem
Bo 7509 – Bo 7810	Ali Dinçol
Bo 7811 – Bo 8187	Sedat Erkut
Bo 8188 – Bo 8506	Muhibbe Darga
Bo 8507 – Bo 8803	Yaşar Coşkun
Bo 8804 – Bo 9097	Yasemin Arıkan
Bo 9098 – Bo 9440	Burhan Balcıoğlu
Bo 9441 – Bo 9736	Nilüfer Boysan

After a period of nearly twenty-five years, some of the members of the team deceased, while some of them retired from academic life or resigned from their duties within the team. After the decision of the Ministry of Culture of the Republic of Turkey in 2010, a new team of Turkish Hittitologists was formed to continue working on the unpublished Bo- fragments, and I received an invitation to become a part of that project. The fragments in question are in the number range of Bo 95 to Bo 9736; the fragments numbered between Bo 9737 and Bo 10296 were determined too small for publication. The fragments are divided among twenty-one Hittitologists, who are partially from the former team, but also younger scholars from various universities and museums in Ankara, Istanbul, Çorum, and Adana. Each team member receives about 170 fragments and is primarily obligated to make hand copies of them. The assignment of the fragments among the current team members is as follows:

Bo 0095 – Bo 3993	Savaş Özkan Savaş
Bo 3994 – Bo 4383	Hasan Peker
Bo 4384 – Bo 4657	Mine Çifçi
Bo 4658 – Bo 5000	Rukiye Akdoğan
Bo 5003 – Bo 5346	Esma Reyhan
Bo 5347 – Bo 5660	İsmet Aykut
Bo 5662 – Bo 7373	Leyla Murat
Bo 5719 – Bo 6086	Aygül Süel
Bo 6087 – Bo 6434	Ahmet Ünal
Bo 6435 – Bo 6842	Cem Karasu
Bo 7374 – Bo 8263	Meltem Doğan Alparslan
Bo 7811 – Bo 8187	Sedat Erkut
Bo 8264 – Bo 8485	İlknur Taş
Bo 8486 – Bo 8694	Metin Alparslan
Bo 8695 – Bo 9535	Başak Yıldız
Bo 8804 – Bo 9097	Yasemin Arıkan

Bo 9098 – Bo 9440	Burhan Balcıoğlu
Bo 9536 – Bo 9736	Oğuz Soysal
Bo 9737 – Bo 10296	(unassigned)

My share includes the range between the numbers Bo 9536 and Bo 9736. In June 2010, when I visited the Ankara Museum to check these fragments, I noted that they are mostly one-sided tiny pieces of a maximum of 10 lines, which are probably not worthy to be copied for a cuneiform publication. However, the fragments can be utilized otherwise and could be useful for Hittite studies. In winter 2010/2011 and summer 2011, I conducted my research in the Ankara Museum, where I took digital pictures of about 500 Bo- fragments. As part of my duties in the CHD-Project, I prepared transliterations of the texts in question, whereby I noticed a number of joins and duplicates. The first results are now found at the *Konkordanz der hethitischen Keilschrifttafeln* (http://www.hethport.uni-wuerzburg.de/hetkonk/) under their relevant text categories, and a related article "Joins, Duplicates, and More from the Unpublished Bo 9000-fragments" was published in the Dutch journal *Anatolica* 38 (2012) 169–90. The photographs, transliterations, and other textual treatments of the entire material are now presented in this monograph entitled *Unpublished Bo-Fragments in Transliteration (Bo 9536 – Bo 9736)* as the second volume of the series CHDS.

The small size of the fragments in question made it particularly difficult to determine the text genres and place them in the text categories assigned in E. Laroche's *Catalogue des textes hittites* (CTH). Nevertheless, after two years of intensive work and with the great support of the Chicago Hittite Dictionary Project's lexical files, it has been possible to discover some duplicates and direct joins to well-known compositions from Boğazköy that certainly enrich the Hittite text corpus. The first group of direct joins was made during the period January–April 2011 while the preliminary transliterations were being prepared:

Bo 9587 + KUB 14.17
Bo 9615 + Bo 8752 + KUB 41.2 + KBo 52.27
Bo 9647 + KUB 35.13
Bo 9673 + KBo 5.3
Bo 9679 + KUB 10.72
Bo 9698 + KUB 23.13
Bo 9712 + KUB 9.32

The re-checking and refining of the text transliterations made between August and November 2012 resulted in six additional direct joins:

Bo 9536 + KBo 48.254
Bo 9537 + KBo 19.74 + KUB 21.5
Bo 9557 + KUB 59.71
Bo 9599 + KUB 58.94
Bo 9605 + Bo 3396
Bo 9628 + KUB 36.75

While this volume was in preparation, the final direct join Bo 9605 + Bo 3396 + KBo 53.308 was discovered in May 2014, of which I was able to take a picture in June 2014 in Ankara and include here.

At the time I began my studies on the Bo-9000 fragments, the work on the fragments was in progress, the following direct joins had already been found by other scholars, as indicated in the *Konkordanz der hethitischen Keilschrifttafeln*:

Bo 9571 + KUB 15.38 + Bo 10125 + Bo 9637 + Bo 9569 (by F. Fuscagni)
Bo 9659 + KUB 36.75 (by S. Görke)
Bo 9708 + KBo 15.14 (by F. Fuscagni; now with my confirmation after collation)

As expected, the fragments dealt with here are mostly of religious nature that have significance especially for rituals and festivals. Surprisingly, however, the text genre "treaties" benefits greatly from the new joins and duplicates of unpublished material as well, e.g., Bo 9537 (CTH 76.B), Bo 9559 (CTH 212), Bo 9561 (CTH 68.N), Bo 9595 (CTH 139), Bo 9663 (CTH 212), and Bo 9673 (CTH 42.A). A few fragments are additions to the important historical compositions: Bo 9587 (CTH 61.II.4), Bo 9698 (CTH 211.4), Bo 9721 (CTH 14.V.C). Two direct joins — Bo 9659 and Bo 9628 — to the Middle Hittite prayer KUB 36.75 + (CTH 374.2.A) illuminate a now obscure passage (II 21′–22′) of this composition. The discovery of the fragments Bo 9650 of the Gilgameš Epic (CTH 341.III.22), Bo 9582 of the Myth of ^{d}LAMMA (CTH 343.7), and Bo 9632 of the Hattian-Hittite bilingual benediction (CTH 736.9) is worth mentioning as well.

After several direct joins are found or suggested based mainly on the work with the lexical files in Chicago, the fragments in question are physically glued either by the museum staff or by myself in my various visits later on in Ankara Museum as far as the fragments are present there. Meanwhile, the glued and enlarged pieces have been re-photographed for this publication. In cases, when pertinent fragments were dispersed in different museums (i.e., in Ankara and Istanbul), hence physically impossible to bring together, I received helpful support from my colleagues from the Akademie der Wissenschaften und der Literatur Mainz (Kommission für den Alten Orient) who have very kindly generated the joins through image processing using the old black & white tablet photos which are in the possession of the Akademie. They are the following texts:

Bo 9537 + KBo 19.74 + KUB 21.5
Bo 9569 + Bo 9637 + KUB 15.33b
Bo 9571 + KUB 15.38 + Bo 10125
Bo 9587 + KUB 14.17
Bo 9647 + KUB 35.13
Bo 9673 + KBo 5.3
Bo 9679 + KUB 10.72
Bo 9698 + KUB 23.13
Bo 9712 + KUB 9.32

I would also like to briefly touch on some technical issues: Since all the fragments are small in size I did not see it as necessary to use centimetric scales on the tablet photos. The measurements are adopted from the inventory records of the Ankara Museum of which accuracy cannot be assured. Due to time restraint and limited ability of the non-professional digital camera used for my work, the results may not always meet the expectation of high quality tablet photos. I believe, however, that the photos selected for this publication are good enough to display the shape of tablets, individual sign forms, and ductus (handwriting) in general, and this makes possible more accurate text datings than those cuneiform documents made by hand copy. Notwithstanding the recent debates on text dating in Hittitology, I dated the fragments to my knowledge and conviction, most of the time, in full agreement with those given at the *Konkordanz der hethitischen Keilschrifttafeln*. Only for a few cases (especially for the extremely small pieces) I preferred my own decision which the reader may agree or disagree with.

My research was supported by several financial grants from the Oriental Institute of the University of Chicago that made it possible for me to travel to Turkey and work in Ankara between 2010 and 2012. I would like to express my sincere thanks to Gil Stein and Theo van den Hout for their interest in, and their support and understanding of, my research beyond the CHD works. I am grateful to the directors of the Museum of Ancient Anatolian Civilizations Melih Aslan (former) and Enver Sağır, the deputy directors Nihal Tırpan (retired) and Emel Yurttagül, the curators İsmet Aykut, Şerife Yılmaz, Filiz Akman, Mine Çifçi, and Başak Yıldız for their constant assistance during my time there. Furthermore, I am indebted to Francesco Fuscagni and Gabriella Stivala (both Mainz) for the image processing of the joins as mentioned above, and Thomas Urban, Leslie Schramer, and Rebecca Cain, who made the publication of this book possible.

Last but not least, let me express the wish to pursue the work with further unpublished Bo-Fragments in near future.

Oğuz Soysal
July 17, 2014, Chicago

LIST OF ABBREVIATIONS

TEXTS, AUTHORS, LITERATURE

ABoT	Kemal, Balkan. *Ankara Arkeoloji Müzesinde bulunan Boğazköy Tabletleri: Boğazköy-Tafeln im archäologischen Museum zu Ankara.* Eski Eserler ve Müzeler Genel Müdürlüğü yayınlarından 3/3. İstanbul: Millî Eğitim Basımevi, 1948
Beckman, The Hittite Gilgamesh	Beckman, Gary M. "The Hittite Gilgamesh." In *The Epic of Gilgamesh: A New Translation, Analogues, Criticism*, edited by Benjamin R. Foster. New York: Norton, 2001
Bo	Inventory numbers of Boğazköy tablets excavated 1906–1912
CHD	*The Hittite Dictionary of the Oriental Institute of the University of Chicago.* Chicago
CHDS	Chicago Hittite Dictionary Supplements. Chicago
CTH	Laroche, Emmanuel. *Catalogue des textes hittites.* Second edition. Paris: Klincksieck, 1971
de Roos, *Votive*	de Roos, Johan. *Hittite Votive Texts.* Publications de l'Institut historique et archéologique néerlandais de Stamboul 109. Leiden: Nederlands Instituut voor het Nabije Oosten, 2007
Dinçol, *Belleten* XLIX/193	Dinçol, A. M. "Ašḫella rituali (CTH 394) ve Hititlerde Salgın Hastalıklara Karşı Yapılan Majik İşlemlere Toplu Bir Bakış." *Belleten. Revue publiée par la Société d'histoire turque* XLIX/193 (1985): 1–40
FHG	Fragments hittites de Genève
FHL	Fragments hittites du Louvre
Friedrich, *SV* I	Friedrich, Johannes. *Staatsverträge des Ḫatti-Reiches in hethitischer Sprache* I. Mitteilungen der Vorderasiatisch-ägyptischen Gesellschaft 31/1. Leipzig: Hinrichs, 1926
Fuscagni, HPMM 6	Fuscagni, Francesco, *Hethitische unveröffentlichte Texte aus den Jahren 1906–1912 in der Sekundärliteratur.* Hethitologie Portal Mainz – Materialien 6. Wiesbaden: Harrassowitz Verlag, 2007
Görke, *Aštu*	Görke, Susanne. *Das Ritual der Aštu (CTH 490). Rekonstruktion und Tradition eines hurritisch-hethitischen Rituals aus Boğazköy/Ḫattuša.* Culture and History of the Ancient Near East 40. Leiden - Boston, 2010
Groddek, DBH 14	Groddek, Detlev. *Hethitische Texte in Transkription: KUB 59.* Dresdner Beiträge zur Hethitologie 14. Wiesbaden, Harrassowitz Verlag, 2004
Groddek, DBH 38	Groddek, Detlev. *Hethitische Texte in Transkription: KUB 48* Dresdner Beiträge zur Hethitologie 38. Wiesbaden, Harrassowitz Verlag, 2012
Groddek-Kloekhorst, DBH 19	Groddek, Detlev, and Alwin Kloekhorst. *Hethitische Texte in Transkription: KBo 35.* Dresdner Beiträge zur Hethitologie 19. Wiesbaden, Harrassowitz Verlag, 2006
Haas, *AoF* 34	Haas, Volkert. "Notizen zu den Ritualen der Frau Allaituraḫi aus Mukiš." *Altorientalische Forschungen* 34/1–2 (2007): 9–36
Haas, *KN*	Haas, Volkert. *Der Kult von Nerik. Ein Beitrag zur hethitischen Religionsgeschichte.* Studia Pohl 4. Rome: Päpstliches Bibelinstitut, 1970
Haas-Wegner, ChS 1/5	Haas, Volkert, and Ilse Wegner. *Die Rituale der Beschwörerinnen* ^{SAL}*ŠU.GI*. Corpus der hurritischen Sprachdenkmäler 1, Abteilung, Texte aus Boğazköy 5. Rome: Multigrafica editrice, 1988

HT	*Hittite Texts in the Cuneiform Character in the British Museum*. London: British Museum, 1920
IBoT 2	Bozkurt, Hatice; Muazzez Çığ; and Hans G. Güterbock. *İstanbul Arkeoloji Müzelerinde Bulunan Boğazköy Tabletleri II. – Boğazköy Tablets in the Archaeological Museums of İstanbul II*. İstanbul: Millî Eğitim Basımevi, 1947
IBoT 3	Çığ, Muazzez, and Hatice Kızılyay (Bozkurt). *İstanbul Arkeoloji Müzelerinde Bulunan Boğazköy Tabletleri III. – Boğazköy Tablets in the Archaeological Museums of İstanbul III*. İstanbul: Maarif Matbaası, 1954
IBoT 4	Eren, Mustafa. *İstanbul Arkeoloji Müzelerinde Bulunan Boğazköy Tabletleri IV - Boğazköy Tablets in the Archaeological Museums of İstanbul IV*. Türk Tarih Kurumu yayınları. VI. dizi. sa. 27. Ankara: Türk Tarih Kurumu Basımevi, 1988
KBo	*Keilschrifttexte aus Boghazköi* (vols. 1–22 are a subseries of WVDOG). Leipzig, Berlin. 1921–
KBo 48	Otten, Heinrich; Christel Rüster; and Gernot Wilhelm. *Keilschrifttexte aus Boghazköi* 48. Berlin: Gebr. Mann Verlag, 2007
KBo 52	Corti, Carlo. *Keilschrifttexte aus Boghazköi* 52. Berlin: Gebr. Mann Verlag, 2009
Konkordanz	Košak, Silvin. *Konkordanz der hethitischen Keilschrifttafeln* http://www.hethport.uni-wuerzburg.de/hetkonk/
KUB	*Keilschrifturkunden aus Boghazköi*. Berlin: Akademie-Verlag, 1921–
Kümmel, StBoT 3	Kümmel, Hans Martin. *Ersatzrituale für den hethitischen König*. Studien zu den Boğazköy-Texten 3. Wiesbaden: Harrassowitz, 1967
Laroche, *Myth.*	Laroche, Emmanuel. *Textes mythologiques hittites en transcription*. Paris, 1965 (part I) and 1968 (part II)
Lebrun, *Hymnes*	Lebrun, René. *Hymnes et Prières Hittites*. Homo Religiosus 4. Louvain-la-Neuve: Centre d'histoire des religions, 1980
Mouton, *Rêves*	Mouton, Alice. *Rêves hittites: contribution à une histoire et une anthropologie du rêve en Anatolie ancienne*. Culture and History of the Ancient Near East 28. Leiden: Brill, 2007
Otten, StBoT 15	Otten, Heinrich. *Materialien zum hethitischen Lexikon*. Studien zu den Boğazköy-Texten 15. Wiesbaden: Harrassowitz, 1971
Puhvel, HED 5	Puhvel, Jaan. *Hittite Etymological Dictionary*, Volume 5: *Words Beginning with L*. Berlin: De Gruyter Mouton, 2001
Roszkowska-Mutschler, DBH 22	Roszkowska-Mutschler, Hanna. *Hethitische Texte in Transkription: Kbo 44*. Dresdner Beiträge zur Hethitologie 22. Wiesbaden, Harrassowitz Verlag, 2007
Soysal, *Anatolica* 38	Soysal, Oğuz. "Joins, Duplicates, and More from the Unpublished Bo 9000-Fragments." *Anatolica* 38 (2012) 169–90
Soysal, *JAOS* 129	Soysal, Oğuz."On Recent Cuneiform Editions of Hittite Fragments (I)." *Journal of the American Oriental Society* 129 (2009): 295–306
Soysal, *HWHT*	Soysal, Oğuz. *Hattischer Wortschatz in hethitischer Textüberlieferung*. Handbuch der Orientalistik, Erste Abteilung, Nahe und der Mittlere Osten 74. Leiden: Brill, 2004
Starke, StBoT 30	Starke, Frank. *Die keilschrift-luwischen Texte in Umschrift*. Studien zu den Boğazköy-Texten 30. Wiesbaden: Harrassowitz, 1985
Trabazo-Groddek, DBH 18	Trabazo, José V. García, and Detlev Groddek. *Hethitische Texte in Transkription: KUB 58*. Dresdner Beiträge zur Hethitologie 18. Wiesbaden, Harrassowitz Verlag, 2005
Ünal, *Ḫantitaššu*	Ünal, Ahmet. *The Hittite Ritual of Ḫantitaššu from the City of Ḫurma Against Troublesome Years*. Ankara: Turkish Historical Society Printing House, 1996
VBoT	Götze, Albrecht. *Verstreute Boghazköi-Texte*. Marburg: Selbstverlag, 1930

GENERAL

abl.	ablative	MS	Middle Script
acc.	accusative	Murš.	Muršili
adj.	adjective	Muw.	Muwatalli
cf.	*confer*, compare	n.	note
coloph.	colophon	N/A	no information available
com.	common (gender)	neut.	neuter
dat.	dative	NH	New Hittite
dupl.	duplicate	nom.	nominative
e.g.	*exempli gratia*, for example	NS	New Script
etc.	*et cetera*, and so forth	obv.	obverse
ENS	Early New Script	OH	Old Hittite
gen.	genitive	OS	Old Script
Hurr.	Hurrian	part.	participle
ibid.	*ibidem*, in the same place	pl.	plural
imp.	imperative	pre-NS	Pre-New Script
inst.	instrumental	pres.	present
iter.	iterative	pret.	preterite
LNH	Late New Hittite	rev.	reverse
LNS	Late New Script	rt. col.	right column
loc.	locative	sg.	singular
lt. col.	left column	sup.	supine
lt. e.	left edge	Šupp.	Šuppiluliuma
MH	Middle Hittite	u. e.	upper edge
mid.	middle (voice)	unkn.	unknown
mng.	meaning	voc.	vocative

UNPUBLISHED Bo-FRAGMENTS IN TRANSLITERATION (Bo 9536 – Bo 9736)

Bo 9536 + KBo 48.254

Description: Cult inventory or festival.

CTH: 530 or 670 "*Fragments divers*."

Dating and Script: NH/LNS.

Remarks: Bo 9536 is a one-sided fragment, and its lines 1′–5′ directly join KBo 48.254:6′–10′ (LNS; according to the *Konkordanz*, however, NS).

Measurements: 2.9 × 2.8 × 1.2 cm.

Bibliography: KBo 48, *Inhaltsverzeichnis*, p. VIII (to KBo 48.254); Groddek, DBH 38, 150–51 (to KBo 48.254).

Bo 9536

KBo 48.254 + Bo 9536

KBo 48.254 + Bo 9536 (detail)

(Line numbers of Bo 9536 are in parentheses)

§ 1′	1′	](-)*x̣*(-)[
	2′	](-)*x̣-x̣*(-)[
	3′	*-i̯]a-u-u̯a-*⌈*z*⌉[*a*?(-)
	4′	^{d}…*-r]i-i̯a*[1)] ⌈NINDA⌉.[GUR$_4$?.RA?
	5′	^{d}…*-r]i*?*-i̯a*[1)] NINDA.GUR$_4$.[RA
§ 2′	6′ (= 1′)	^{URU}*N]e-rị-ịk*[2)] ^{d}U ^{URU}*N*⌈*e*⌉*-*[*ri*?*-ik*?
	7′ (= 2′)	*-a]š̌*? [3)] ^{URU}*Ḫa-l*⌈*e*⌉*-*⌊*e*⌋*n-zu-u̯a* ^{d}*Zi-ịt-*[*ḫa-ri-i̯a*(-)[4)]
	8′ (= 3′)	] DÙ*-an-zi*[5)] [
§ 3′	9′ (= 4′)	] ^{URU}*Ne-ri-ik* ^{URU}⌈^{U}⌉[*Ḫ*]*a-le-en-zu-*[*u̯a*
	10′ (= 5′)	]-⌊*z*⌋*u*?*-u* EZEN$_4$*-ŠU* DÙ*-ạn-zi*[5)] [
	11′ (= 6′)	*-a*]*n-zi* [
§ 4′	12′ (= 7′)	]-⌊*x-u̯*⌋*a-zạ a-ri-i̯a-x̣-*[
	13′ (traces?)	
	(broken off)	

Text-critical notes: [1)] Perhaps to be restored with the phrase *A-NA* … ^{d}*Zi-it-ḫa-ri-i̯a* NINDA.GUR$_4$.RA; cf. KUB 56.56 IV 11. [2)] Thus, not [^{d}U ^{URU}*Pít-ti-i̯a-ri*]*-ik* as suggested in KBo 48 *Inhaltsverzeichnis*, p. VIII and Groddek, DBH 38, 151. [3)] The clear horizontal sign reminder excludes the possibility of [^{d}LAMM]A ^{URU}*Ḫa-l*⌈*e*⌉*-*⌊*e*⌋*n-zu-u̯a* as proposed in KBo 48, *Inhaltsverzeichnis*, p. VIII, and Groddek, DBH 38, 151. [4)] For a co-attestation of ^{d}Zitḫariya and ^{URU}Ḫalenzuwa see IBoT 3.11:1′, 4′–5′. [5)] The (L)NH use of DÙ*-anzi* "they celebrate" suggests a cult inventory text here rather than a festival description.

Bo 9537 + KBo 19.74 + KUB 21.5

Description: Treaty.

CTH: 76.B "*Traité avec Alaksandu de Wiluša.*"

Dating and Script: Muw. II/NS.

Remarks: Bo 9537 is a moderately abraded fragment, and its lines 1′–7′ directly join KBo 19.74 + KUB 21.5 IV 7–13 (NS). Bo 9537 + KBo 19.74 + KUB 21.5 IV 7–14 are duplicate of KUB 21.1+ III 73–83 (NS) and HT 8:1′–7′ (NS), from where the restorations are taken.

Measurements: 3.0 × 2.1 × 0.4 cm.

Bibliography: N/A.

Bo 9537

KBo 19.74 + Bo 9537 rev. IV (KUB 21.5 is not included)

Bo 9537 + KBo 19.74 + KUB 21.5 rev. IV (composite image)

Reverse IV
(Line numbers of Bo 9537 are in parentheses)

§ 2 7 (= 1′) [(nam-ma ki-i ku-it ṬU)]P-PU tu-u̯k A-NA[1)] ^{m}A-la-ak-ša-a[n]-⸢du⸣ i-i̯a-nu-un

8 (= 2′) [(ne-et-ták-kán MU)-t]i MU-ti[2)] pí-ra-an 3-ŠÚ ḫạl-zi-ša-[a]n-du n˻a-a˼[(t-za)]-kán zi-ik

9 (= 3′) [(^{m}A-la-ak-ša-an-du-uš)] ša-ki-iš-ši[3)] ke-e-ma[4)] A-WA-TE^{MEŠ} Ú-UL ku-ị[(t-k)i]

10 (= 4′) [(I-e-da-az I-e-da-az)] IŠ-TỤ KUR ^{URU}Ḫa-at-ti-at nu zị-ik ^{m}Ạ-ḷ[(a-ak-ša-an-du-uš)]

11 (= 5′) [(IT-TI ^{d}UTU-ŠI ḪUL-lu)] ⸢Ú-UL i-i̯a-ši tu-uk-ma-kán ^{URU}Ḫa-at-tụ[5)]-ṣ[a-aš ḪUL-lu]

12 (= 6′) [(Ú-UL ták-ke-e-e)]š-zi nu ka-a-aš-ma a-pé-e-dạ-[n]i me-mi-i̯a-an-n[i[6)] ^{d}UTU-ŠI]

13 (= 7′) [^{m}La-ba-a(r-na-aš LUGAL.GAL NA)]-˻RA˼-ẠM ^{d}U pí-ḫa-aš-ša-ši L[I-I]˻M˼ DINGIR.MEŠ tu-l[i-i̯a ḫ(al-zi-iḫ-ḫu-un)]

14 (= 8′) [(na-aš ku-ut-ru-u̯a-aḫ-ḫu-u)n n(u i)]⸢š-ta?⸣-[(ma-aš-kán-d)]u uš-ká[n[7)]-du-i̯a(?)]

(broken off)

Text-critical notes: [1)] Duplicate KUB 21.1+ III 73 omits A-NA. [2)] Duplicates KUB 21.1+ III 74 and HT 8:1′: MU.KAM-ti MU.KAM-ti. [3)] KUB 21.1+ III 75: ša-kị. [4)] KUB 21.1+ III 76: ki-i-ma. [5)] KUB 21.1+ III 79: -du-. [6)] The signs -an-n[i] are written with a small script curving down over an erasure. [7)] The first two signs as seen in Bo 9537 line 6′ are not very clear, but definitely not to be read iš-t[a-…].

Bo 9538

Description: Festival.

CTH: 670 "*Fragments divers.*"

Dating and Script: NS.

Remarks: One-sided fragment.

Measurements: 2.5 × 3.0 × 0.5 cm.

Bibliography: N/A.

Bo 9538

§ 1′ 1′] ⸢III? DUG? *x x x*⸣ [
2′] *nu-kán* I UDU Ạ-[*NA*(?)[1)]
3′] Ị? ỤDU-*ma-kán* [
4′ *š*]*i-pạ-an-ti* *x̣*(-)[
5′](-)*x̣*?-*x̣* ḪUR.SẠG(./-)[
6′ (traces)
(broken off)

Text-critical note: [1)] Lines 2′–4′ are to be reconstructed as *nu=kan* I UDU *A*[*NA* ᵈ…] / I UDU-*ma=kan* [*A-NA* ᵈ…] / [*š*]*ipanti*, which would refer to a festival including animal sacrifices.

Bo 9539

Description: Festival.

CTH: 670 "*Fragments divers.*"

Dating and Script: N/A, however, the script appears to be older than NS.

Remarks: One-sided fragment that seems to be part of a six-column tablet. As far as preserved, the tablet consists mostly of short paragraphs of two lines with identical descriptions. For similar context, see various festivals: KBo 11.22 obv. III 1–21 (CTH 656.2.A), KBo 17.9+ I 2′–13′ (627.1.h.A), KBo 22.195+ I[!] 3′–15′ (CTH 627.1.h.B), KBo 33.165+ I 1′–15′ II 1′–13′ (CTH 628), KBo 33.215+ V 2′–24′, VI 1′–19′ (CTH 628), KBo 25.60(+) III 2′–11′ (CTH 669.30), KUB 27.1 IV 25–44 (CTH 712.A).

Measurements: 3.9 × 3.2 × 0.8 cm.

Bibliography: N/A.

Bo 9539

Left column

§ 1′	1′	-*z*]⸢*i*⸣[1]
	2′	SÌ]R-*RU*
§ 2′	3′	]-*zi*
	4′	SÌ]R-*RU*
§ 3′	5′	]-*x̣*-*zi*
	6′	SÌR-*R*]*U*
§ 4′	7′	]- *aš*[2]
	(broken off)	

Right column

§ 1′	1′	⸢EGIR⸣-[*ŠU-ma*
	2′	^{GIŠ}*ḫal*$^{?}$ [3]-[
§ 2′	3′	EGIR-*Š*[*U-ma*
	4′	$^{\text{LÚ.ME}}$[^{Š}
§ 3′	5′	EGI[R-*ŠU-ma*
	6′	^{GI}[^{Š}
§ 4′	7′	E[GIR-*ŠU-ma*(?)[4]
	(broken off)	

Text-critical notes: [1] The predicate in the end of the lines 1′, 3′, and 5′ is most likely *e-ku-zi*. [2] Restore [TUŠ]-*aš* or [GUB]-*aš*. [3] Although two signs read rather ^{GIŠ}*ḫal-*, a different interpretation, like GIŠ.⸢^{d}⸣[INANNA.GAL/TUR], cannot be excluded here. [4] The reciprocal restorations of the left and right columns show the following formula: EGIR-*ŠU⸗ma* LUGAL-*uš* TUŠ/GUB-*aš* ^{d}... *ekuzi* (NINDA.GUR$_4$.RA *paršiya*)$^{?}$ GIŠ.^{d}INANNA.GAL/TUR $^{\text{LÚ.MEŠ}}$... SÌR-*RU*.

Bo 9541

Description: Cult inventory.

CTH: 522 "*Descriptions de statues, idoles, objets divers: fragments.*"

Dating and Script: NH/NS.

Remarks: One-sided fragment from the right side (with edge) of a tablet.

Measurements: 2.8 × 2.6 × 1.2 cm.

Bibliography: N/A.

Bo 9541

Bo 9541 (right edge)

§ 1′ 1′ [^{d}…]-*u̯a̯*[1)]

2′] *ku̯-ru-ta-a-u-u̯a-an-za*

3′ *pár-ka$_4^?$-aš*]-*ti* *ŠA* I SIG.KÙŠ 1/2 SI[G.KÙŠ[2)]]

4′ G]UN$^?$

5′ (traces)

(broken off)

Text-critical notes: [1)] Lines 1′ ff. belong to the description of a divine image. [2)] For restorations, see KUB 38.3 I 10 and 19.

Bo 9542

Description: Hurrian lists of offerings.

CTH: 787 *"Listes d'offrandes."*

Dating and Script: MH/MS$^{?}$.

Remarks: One-sided fragment that is duplicate or parallel to KBo 35.246+ rev. 18′–19′ (CTH 787), from where the restorations are taken. Cf. similar lists also in KBo 45.254 I 10′–12′ (CTH 706.II), KBo 46.102 I 33′–36′ (CTH 615.13), and KUB 27.8 obv. 12′–15′ (CTH 704.2.A).

Measurements: 2.9 × 2.4 × 1.0 cm.

Bibliography: N/A.

Bo 9542

§ 1′ …

———

§ 2′ 1′ EGIR-*p*⸢*a-m*⸣[*a* 1 NINDA.SIG *A-NA* ^{d}*Ša-a?-la-aš* ^{d}*Pé-e?-te-en-ḫi*]

2′ *pár-ši-i̯*⸢*a*⸣ [KI.MIN]

---

§ 3′ 3′ Ẹ̣GIR-*pa-m*[*a* 1 NINDA.SIG *A-NA* ^{d}*A-dam-ma* ^{d}*Ku-pa-pa*]

4′ ^{ḍ}*Ḫa-šu-u*[*n-tar-ḫi pár-ši-i̯a* KI.MIN]

---

§ 4′ 5′ [EGIR-*p*]⸤*a-ma*⸥ [

(broken off)

Bo 9543

Description: List of rations$^{?}$.

CTH: 677$^{?}$ "*Fragments de listes de 'rations'* (*tarnattas*)."

Dating and Script: NS.

Remarks: Tiny, one-sided fragment.

Measurements: 3.2 × 3.1 × 0.7 cm.

Bibliography: N/A.

Bo 9543

§ 1′	1′	](-)*x̣*(-)⸢*x-x*⸣(-)[
	2′	^{DU}]^{G}*ḫa-ni-i*⸢*š*⸣-[*ša*(-)
	3′	*š*]*u*$^{?}$-*un-na-an-tẹ*-[*eš*[1]
	4′	*z*]*ị*$^{?}$-*nạ*$^{?}$-*ịl*(-)[2]⸤*x*⸥-[
	5′	]*x̣*.⸤MEŠ⸥ *x̣-x̣*$^{?}$(-)[
	(broken off)	

Text-critical notes: [1] If this reading is correct, the part. pl. nom. com. form *šunnanteš* to *šunna-* "to fill" is attested for the first time here (based on the information from the CHD files). [2] The word *zinail-* would refer to the context in IBoT 2.93 obv. 14′–16′, KBo 11.41 I 8′–10′, Bo 3123 IV 6′–8′ (// KBo 25.79 IV$^{?}$ 6′–8′), KUB 42.107 obv. III$^{?}$ 11′–12′ (all to CTH 677) where $^{(DUG)}$*ḫanešša*(*r*)- (Bo 9543:2′) is also present.

Bo 9544

Description: Ritual.

CTH: 470 "*Fragments de rituels.*"

Dating and Script: NS.

Remarks: One-sided fragment.

Measurements: 2.2 × 2.5 × 0.9 cm.

Bibliography: N/A.

Bo 9544

§ 1′ 1′]⸢*x̣-x̣*⸣[
2′]-⸢*zi*⸣ [
3′ MUNUSŠ]⸢U.G⸣I *kiš-a*[*n*[1)]
4′]-*x̣ ud-da-a-ạr*(-)[
5′ -*a*]*n*?-*ta-ru* [
6′](-)⸤*mi-x-x*⸥(-)[
(broken off)

Text-critical note: [1)] One expects here a verb like *te-*, *mema-*, or *ḫuek-*, thus the following lines may contain the conjuration / recitation of the here-mentioned Old Woman.

Bo 9545

Description: N/A.

CTH: 832 "*Fragments en langue hittite de nature inconnue.*"

Dating and Script: LNS.

Remarks: One-sided fragment that is too small to classify.

Measurements: 3.0 × 2.5 × 1.1 cm.

Bibliography: N/A.

Bo 9545

§ 1′	1′	] ⌈*x̣*⌉-[
	2′	(-)*ḫ*]*a-an-na-x̣*(-)[1)][
	3′	]-*x̣* *nu-u̯a-x̣*(-)[
	4′	] *a-pí-i̯*[*a*(-)
§ 2′	5′	(traces)
		(broken off)

Text-critical note: [1)] If this word can be related to the verb *ḫanna-* "to judge, " one may compare the context of KUB 30.24+ II 2–5 (CTH 450.I), which contain the words *ḫannari* (II 2), *nu=wa=šši=kan* (II 3), and *apiya* (II 5), apparently in the same order as in Bo 9545:2′–4′. That these texts are duplicates, however, cannot be claimed yet with certainty.

Bo 9547

Description: N/A.

CTH: 832 "*Fragments en langue hittite de nature inconnue.*"

Dating and Script: NS.

Remarks: One-sided fragment that is too small to classify.

Measurements: 3.1 × 2.8 × 1.1 cm.

Bibliography: N/A.

Bo 9547

§ 1′ …

——

§ 2′ 1′] *ŠA* [

————————

§ 3′ 2′ *ku*]-⸢*i*⸣*š im-m*[*a ku-iš*(?)[1)]

3′ *n*]*a-ạt-ta ku-i*[*š*?-*ki*?

4′](-)⸤*x*⸥-*pát ạ*-⸤*x*⸥-[

5′ (traces)

(broken off)

Text-critical note: [1)] The expression *kuiš imma kuiš* and the negation in the following line would hint at an instructive / directive context, e.g., treaty, protocol, instruction, etc.

Bo 9548

Description: Ritual or festival.

CTH: 470 "*Fragments de rituels*" or 670 "*Fragments divers.*"

Dating and Script: NS.

Remarks: One-sided fragment in which the lines are written askew.

Measurements: 2.1 × 3.1 × 1.2 cm.

Bibliography: N/A.

Bo 9548

§ 1′ 1′ *-m*]⌈*a*⌉*-aš-*⌈*ša-a*⌉[*n*

2′ $^{UZU?}$*ḫu-uḫ-ḫ*]*ụ-ur-ti-i*⌈*š*⌉*-x̣*$^{?}$(-)[1)][

3′ *-a*]*š*$^{?}$ *šu-uḫ-ḫa*(-)*a*[*n-*[2)]

---

§ 2′ 4′]⌊*x x x x x x*⌋[

(broken off)

Text-critical notes: [1)] $^{(UZU)}$*ḫuḫḫurti-* "throat" seems to be extant also in KBo 32.106 rev.$^{?}$ 8′ as incomplete *ḫu-uḫ-ḫu-*[…]. My early attempt to join Bo 9548 lines 1′–3′ and KBo 32.106 rev.$^{?}$ 7′–9′ (MS) through the word *ḫuḫḫurtiš* has failed after a collation from the photo of KBo 32.106. Moreover, both fragments exhibit different script and ductus. [2)] Either verbal *šu-uḫ-ḫa-a*[*n-zi*$^{?}$] "[they] scatter" or nominal *šu-uḫ-ḫa a*[*n-da*$^{?}$] "i[nto] the roof."

Bo 9549

Description: N/A.

CTH: 832 "*Fragments en langue hittite de nature inconnue.*"

Dating and Script: NS.

Remarks: One-sided fragment that is too small to classify.

Measurements: 3.8 × 3.2 × 1.4 cm.

Bibliography: N/A.

Bo 9549

§ 1′ 1′ (traces)

2′]-*x̣-za*? *x̣*-[

3′](.)x̣.MEŠ? [1)] *x̣*-[

4′]-*x̣* *a-pí-ịz*-[

5′](-)*x̣-e-še*?-*x̣*(-)[

6′ (-)*t*]*a*?-*i̯a*-⌜*z*⌝[*i*?

7′].⌞M⌟EŠ? [1)] *x̣*-[

(broken off)

Text-critical note: [1)] Alternatively, to be read: *x̣-eš*.

Bo 9550

Description: Cult inventory.

CTH: 530 "*Fragments divers.*"

Dating and Script: NH/LNS.

Remarks: One-sided fragment.

Measurements: 3.3 × 3.4 × 1.0 cm.

Bibliography: N/A.

Bo 9550

§ 1′ 1′] ⸢NINDA?⸣.x̣(./-)[

2′ -*z*]*i-i̯*⸢*a*⸣ [

3′]

---

§ 2′ 4′] NỊNDA.GUR$_4$.RA *li-la-aš*(-)[1)][

---

§ 3′ 5′ *P*]*A*? ZÌ.DA *še-pí-tàš*[2)] [

6′] Ị? *UP-NU* BA.BA.ZA NINDA.G[UR$_4$?.RA?

7′ (traces)

(broken off)

Text-critical notes: [1)] *lila-* "conciliation" is a common word for the cult inventory texts (see CHD L–N/1 [1980] 57 and Puhvel, HED 5, 77–78) but its co-attestation with NINDA.GUR$_4$.RA is noted only here. [2)] This is a rare spelling for *šepit*(*t*)*aš*.

Bo 9553

Description: Festival.

CTH: 670 "*Fragments divers.*"

Dating and Script: NS.

Remarks: One-sided, slightly abraded fragment from the left portion (with edge) of a tablet.

Measurements: 3.2 × 1.7 × 1.5 cm.

Bibliography: N/A.

Bo 9553

§ 1′ 1′ *nu-za* LỤ́[

2′ *nụ e-ẹš*̌?-[

3′ *pí-rạ-a*[*n*

---

§ 2′ 4′ ỤDU *a*[*r-kán-zi*(?)[1)]

5′ ỤZUZẠG.Ụ[DU(-)

6′ *pị́-rạ-a*[*n*

---

§ 3′ 7′ […]⌊*x-x*⌋[

(broken off)

Text-critical note: [1)] On this simple syntax (without any phonetic complement and particle *=kan*), cf. KBo 38.65:5′ (CTH 670.291): GU_4.MAḪ *a-a*[*r-kán-zi*], likewise opening a new paragraph.

Bo 9554

Description: Ritual or festival.

CTH: 470 "*Fragments de rituels*" or 670 "*Fragments divers.*"

Dating and Script: NS.

Remarks: One-sided fragment, the right edge of which is also inscribed.

Measurements: 3.1 × 1.6 × 2.3 cm.

Bibliography: N/A.

Bo 9554

Bo 9554 (right edge)

§ 1′ 1′ (traces)

2′] *ḫạ-ad-du-l*[*a-a*$^{?}$*-tar*$^{?}$ $^{1)}$]

3′]-*ạr*

4′]-*x̣* ⌈*x-x-x-x-x*⌋ (erasure)

5′](-)*un-na-an-z*[*i*]

6′ .Ḫ]I.A

7′ *UŠ-K*]*É-EN*

(broken off)

Text-critical note: $^{1)}$ The incomplete nouns *ḫaddul*[*ātar*] here and [...]*ar* in the following line may be part of a benediction speech in course of this ritual / festival.

Bo 9555

Description: Festival.

CTH: 670 "*Fragments divers.*"

Dating and Script: OH/OS.

Remarks: Small, one-sided fragment that has writing on its curved portion.

Measurements: 2.4 × 2.3 × 2.1 cm.

Bibliography: N/A.

Bo 9555

§ 1′ 1′ (traces)
2′ -*ḫ*]*a-an-*⸢*zi*?⸣[

---

§ 2′ 3′]-*x̣*? *I-NẠ* É d?*x*(./-)[
4′ LÚSAG]I.A(?) *zi-nịr*(-)*x̣*?(-)[1)][
5′]-*x̣-kur*? *x̣*-[
6′ (traces)
(broken off)

Text-critical note: [1)] Probably to be read *zi-nịr*(-)*z*[*i-nir*].

Bo 9556

Description: Festival.

CTH: 670 "*Fragments divers.*"

Dating and Script: NS.

Remarks: Small, one-sided fragment.

Measurements: 2.9 × 2.2 × 1.3 cm.

Bibliography: N/A.

Bo 9556

§ 1′ …

—

§ 2′ 1′ -*š*]*a*$^{?}$-*az*$^{!?}$ *i-i̯*[*a*$^{?}$-

2′] III-*ŠU* [

3′ GIŠ.]^{d}̣INANNA.GAL [

---

§ 3′ 4′ ^{d}…]-*il*[1)] ^{d}*Zạ-l*[*i*$^{?}$-

5′ ^{d}…]-*šị-i* ⸤^{d}⸥[

(broken off)

Text-critical note: [1)] All nominal features indicate that a Hattian divine circle is present in this paragraph. For the divine proper names here, cf. the passage in KUB 53.44 obv. III 5′–7′ (CTH 647.16): DUMU.LUGAL GUB-*aš* ^{d}*Tu-ḫ*[*a-a*$^{?}$-*ša-il* …$^{?}$] / ^{d}*Za-li-nu-un* ^{d}*Ḫ*[*a-ra-at-ši-i*°(?) *e-ku-zi*] / GIŠ^{d}ỊNANNA.GAL […].

Bo 9557 + KUB 59.71

Description: Ritual.

CTH: 780.II.1.T.A "*Rituel d'Allaituraḫi*."

Dating and Script: MH/NS.

Remarks: Bo 9557 is a one-sided fragment, and its lines 1′–6′ directly join KUB 59.71 I 11–16 (NS). Bo 9557 + KUB 59.71 I 11–16 are duplicate to KUB 12.53(+)KUB 58.107 I 6′–11′ (NS) and KBo 35.118 l. col. 4′–8′ (NS), from where the restorations are taken.

Measurements: 3.3 × 4.2 × 0.8 cm.

Bibliography: Haas-Wegner, ChS I/5, 67 (Nr. 3) (to KUB 59.71 without join), 72 (Nr. 5) (to dupl. KUB 12.53), 74 (Nr. 6) (to dupl. KBo 35.118, then unpublished 968/v); Groddek, DBH 14, 122 (to KUB 59.71 without join); Trabazo-Groddek, DBH 18, 269 (to dupl. KUB 58.107(+) KUB 12.53); Groddek-Kloekhorst, DBH 19, 137 (to dupl. KBo 35.118); Haas, *AoF* 34, 12 (to KUB 59.71 and its duplicates).

Bo 9557

KUB 59.71 + Bo 9557 obv. I

KUB 59.71 + Bo 9557 obv. I (detail)

Obverse I

(Line numbers of Bo 9557 are in parentheses)

§ 3 11 (= 1′) [(*na-aš-ma* XV GÍN URUDU)] *da-an-zi* I ^{SÍG}*ḳi-ịš-rị-ịš*(-)*x̣*(-)[…$^{?}$-(*ši*$^{?}$) [1]]

12 (= 2′) [(NINDA.SIG.MEŠ XII ^{NINDA}*za-pa-ḫi* ^{NINDA}*ša-la*)]-*kar ta-lu-kán* IỊI *UP-NI*

13 (= 3′) [(III ^{NINDA}*zi-ip-pé-en-ni-i*)]*š* III *UP-NU* ZÌ.Ḍ[A.ZÍ]Z$^{?}$ *nu ku-iš-ša*

14 (= 4′) [*ŠA* (1/2 *UP-NI*)][2) [ ]

---

§ 2′ 15 (= 5′) [… (I$^{?}$ GÍR)(.) …[3)] (III *NAM-MA-A*)]*N-DU*$_4$ Ì.NU[(N)] II DUG *QA-TÙ* Ì.DÙG.GA […$^{?}$]

16 (= 6′) [*ku-i*(*š-ša ŠA* 1/2 *UP-NI* I GADA)] ŠU.MEŠ-*a*[(*š*)][4)] I-*NU*-⌊*T*⌋*Ì* GIŠ.RÍN ZI.BA.N[(A) …$^{?}$]

(Bo 9557 breaks here off; KUB 59.71 has one more line with illegible sign remnants)

Text-critical notes: [1)] Not very certain if […]-*ši*$^{?}$ in the duplicate KUB 12.53(+)KUB 58.107 I 10′ is to be placed here. [2)] As the recent join shows, this line appears to be inscribed. Thus, contrary to the edition in KUB 59, it should be numbered as "14." [3)] Against the restoration made by Haas, *AoF* 34, 12, there is not enough space for a "ZABAR" (= "UD.KA.BAR") in the broken part in KUB 12.53(+)KUB 58.107 I 10′ between the signs "GÍR" and "III." [4)] KUB 12.53(+)KUB 58.107 I 11′: ŠU-*aš*.

Bo 9559

Description: Treaty / protocol or instruction / oath.

CTH: 212 "*Traités* (*ou protocoles*): *fragments*" or 275 "*Fragments de protocoles* (*ou de traités ?*)."

Dating and Script: NS.

Remarks: One-sided fragment.

Measurements: 2.07 × 2.6 × 0.7 cm.

Bibliography: N/A.

Bo 9559

§ 1′ 1′ *p*]⸢*í-ra-a*⸣[*n*

2′]-*u̯a-i̯a-a*[*n*(-)

3′] *ạr-ḫa ú-*[

4′ *N*]*I-IŠ* DINGIR.MEŠ *QA-*[*DU …-KU-NU*(?)

5′]-*x̣ pa-an-ku-ni-i*[*t*

6′ *A-NA …*]-*KỤ-NU A-NA* KUR-*KU-N*[*U*[1)]

7′ -*k*]*án-* *zi* [

---

§ 2′ 8′ (traces)

(broken off)

Text-critical note: [1)] For *ANA* KUR-*KUNU* "to your (pl.) land," see KUB 23.72+ rev. 63. Lines 4′–7′, containing also the term *NĪŠ* DINGIR.MEŠ "oath-deities," seem to be a cursing section at the end of the paragraph.

Bo 9560

Description: Soldier's oath$^{?}$.

CTH: 427 "*Le 'serment' militaire.*"

Dating and Script: MH/MS$^{?}$ or pre-NS$^{?}$.

Remarks: Bo 9560 is a one-sided fragment, and its lines 2′–5′ appear to duplicate KBo 6.34 + II 27–31. Although the matching four lines may suggest the proposal made here, this cannot be fully confirmed.

Measurements: 2.2 × 2.5 × 1.0 cm.

Bibliography: N/A.

Bo 9560

§ 1′ 1′]-*x̣* ⌈*x-an*$^{?}$⌉(-)[
2′ -*k*]*i*$^{?}$-*id-du*[1] ⌈*x*⌋(erasure) [
3′]-*x̣* *da-ra-a*[*n-zi*$^{?}$[2]
4′ -*e*]*š̌*$^{?}$- *du*[3] [

---

§ 2′ 5′ *m*]*a*$^{?}$-*aḫ-ḫa-an*[4] [
(broken off)

Text-critical notes: [1] Cf. KBo 6.34+ II 27: *i-nu-uš-ki-du.* [2] Cf. KBo 6.34+ II 29: *a-pé-e-ma da-ra-an-zi.* [3] Cf. KBo 6.34+ II 30: *e-eš-du.* [4] Cf. KBo 6.34+ II 31: GIM-*an*.

Bo 9561

Description: Treaty.

CTH: 68.N "*Traité avec Kupanta-ᵈKAL du pays de Mira et Kuwaliya.*"

Dating and Script: Murš. II/NS.

Remarks: Bo 9561 is a one-sided fragment, and its lines 4′–6′ appear to duplicate KUB 19.52 IV? (Friedrich, *SV* I, § 30†† J) 1′–3′, from where the restorations are taken.

Measurements: 2.5 × 3.4 × 1.1 cm.

Bibliography: Soysal, *Anatolica* 38, 174 (transliteration and remarks).

Bo 9561

§ 1′ 1′ *p*]⸢*í*?-*i̯a-an-du*?⸣[1)][

2′ -*š*]*i*? [

3′ …

---

§ 2′ 4′ (*i-i̯*)]*a-nu-un* [

5′ (*ḫal-z*)]*e-eš-kán-d*[(*u*)[2)]]

6′ (*p*)]*a-ạḫ-ši* [

7′ (traces)

(broken off)

Text-critical notes: [1)] Or less probably ⸢*u-i̯a-an-du*?⸣. [2)] KUB 19.52 IV? 2′: *ḫal-zi-iš-kán-d*⸢*u*⸣.

Bo 9562

Description: N/A.

CTH: 832 "*Fragments en langue hittite de nature inconnue.*"

Dating and Script: NS.

Remarks: One-sided fragment that is too small to classify; perhaps of historical or instructive nature.

Measurements: 2.3 × 3.3 × 1.4 cm.

Bibliography: N/A.

Bo 9562

§ 1′ 1′]⸢*x* *x-x*⸣[

2′]-*x̣* ŠẸŠ-*m*⸢*a*$^{?}$⸣(-)*x̣*$^{?}$(-)[

3′ *p*]*é*$^{?}$-*e-dạ-ạn*(-) [

4′ *A-N*]*A*(?) ^{d}ỤTU-*ŠỊ*(?) *up-pa-ụ́*$^{?}$ [

---

§ 2′ 5′ (traces$^{?}$)

(broken off)

Bo 9563

Description: Festival.

CTH: 670 "*Fragments divers.*"

Dating and Script: NS$^{?}$; some sign forms ("BAL" and "LAMMA"), however, appear to be a bit older.

Remarks: One-sided fragment from the right side (with edge) of a tablet.

Measurements: 3.4 × 3.2 × 1.3 cm.

Bibliography: N/A.

Bo 9563

§ 1′ 1′]-x̣
2′ -t]i
3′]-zi

---

§ 2′ 4′ *A-NA* DINGIR$^{?}$].MEŠ BẠL-*ti*

---

§ 3′ 5′ *A-N*]*A*(?) ^{d}LAMMA [
6′ …

---

§ 4′ 7′ *A-N*]⸤*A*(?) $^{d?}$⸥[
(broken off)

Bo 9564

Description: N/A.

CTH: 831 "*Fragments en langue inconnue ou indéterminée.*"

Dating and Script: N/A.

Remarks: One-sided fragment that is too small to classify.

Measurements: 4.2 × 1.2 × 2.6 cm.

Bibliography: N/A.

Bo 9564

§ 1′	1′	(-)*p*]*ur*?-[
	2′	]-*x̣*-*x̣*(-)[
§ 2′	3′	-*z*]*i*(-)[
§ 3′	4′	]-*ụn*(-)[
	5′	]-*x̣*-*r*[*i*?(-)
	6′	]⸢*x*⸣[

(broken off)

Bo 9565

Description: N/A.

CTH: 832 "*Fragments en langue hittite de nature inconnue*."

Dating and Script: N/A.

Remarks: One-sided fragment of the edge portion of a tablet that is too small to classify.

Measurements: 3.1 × 2.7 × 1.4 cm.

Bibliography: N/A.

Bo 9565

Bo 9565 (right edge)

§ 1′ 1′]-⸢*x̣-a*⸣*n*$^{?}$-*zị*
2′]-*x̣-šị-iš*
3′ …
4′]-*ẹ-eš*
5′ -*z*]*i-pa-aš*[1)]
(broken off)

Text-critical note: [1)] This word may belong either to the lemmata *daganzipa-* "ground" or *taršanzipa-* "platform$^{?}$," or to a divine proper name with final element *-zipa*.

Bo 9566

Description: Festival.

CTH: 670 “*Fragments divers.*”

Dating and Script: NS.

Remarks: One-sided fragment that is perhaps part of a six-column tablet.

Measurements: 3.2 × 3.2 × 1.0 cm.

Bibliography: N/A.

Bo 9566

Left column

§ 1′	1′	^{GIŠ}DÌ]M[1)]
	2′	^{GIŠ}D]ÌM[1)]
	3′	-*z*]*a*$^{?}$
	(broken off)	

Right column

§ 1′	1′	UGULA ^{L}[$^{\text{Ú.MEŠ(?)}}$
	2′	*ḫu-ụ-*[*u̯a-a*$^{?}$*-i*
	3′	*na-x̣*(-)[
§ 2′	4′	*nu-z*[*a*
	5′	⸢*x*⸣[
	(broken off)	

Text-critical note: [1)] Logogram ^{GIŠ}DÌM “pillar” as occurs in the festivals (mostly from the Hattian milieu), see KBo 23.56 IV$^{?}$ 6′ (CTH 647); KBo 45.129 V 20′ (CTH 738.I.31); KUB 27.70+ III 18′, 20′ (CTH 681.1); KUB 53.3 lt. e. 2 (CTH 638.2.I); IBoT 4.137 II 3′ (CTH 670.1659).

Bo 9567

Description: N/A.

CTH: 832 "*Fragments en langue hittite de nature inconnue*."

Dating and Script: NS.

Remarks: One-sided fragment that is too small to classify.

Measurements: 4.5 × 3.5 × 0.9 cm.

Bibliography: N/A.

Bo 9567

§ 1′	1′	]⸢*x̣*⸣[
	2′	](-)⸤*t*⸥*u-l*⸢*i-x̣*⸣(-)[
§ 2′	3′	*Š*]*A-ME-E x̣*(-)[
	4′	] *nu-u̯a k*[*u-*
	5′	]*-tar nu* [
	6′	*Ú-U*]*L*(?) *ku-ịt-*[*ki*
	7′	*-u̯*]*a*?*-an x̣-*[
	8′	*-t*]*a*? *nu-u̯*[*a*?(-)
	9′	]-⸤*x̣-zi*⸥(-)[

(broken off)

Bo 9568

Description: Cult inventory.

CTH: 530 "*Fragments divers.*"

Dating and Script: NH/NS or LNS.

Remarks: One-sided fragment.

Measurements: 2.5 × 2.8 × 0.7 cm.

Bibliography: N/A.

Bo 9568

§ 1′	1′	*-z]i*[?] ⸢*du-uš-ka*$_4$*-ra*⸣-[*az*[?]
	2′	*-i̯]a* ^{GIŠ}ZAG.GAR.RA *x̣*-[
	3′	(-)*p]a-an-zi*[1)] LIBIR-*RU-ma*(-)[
	4′	]-*x̣ ti-i̯a-an-zi* GI[M-*an*(-)
	5′	DINGIR-*L*]*UM kar-ap-pa-an-z*[*i*[2)]
	6′	*pa*[? 3)]*-r*]*a-a ú-d*⸤*a-*⸥*an-*[*zi*
	7′	]-*x̣* ⸤*pí-x̣*⸥-[
	(broken off)	

Text-critical notes: [1)] Possibly: [*kar-ap-p*]*a-an-zi*. [2)] For restoration, see KBo 2.7 obv. 16′ (CTH 505.1). [3)] Or: [*ša-r*]*a-a*.

Bo 9569 + Bo 9637 + KUB 15.33b +

Description: Evocation ritual.

CTH: 483.II.A "*Rituel: quand on tire les dieux sur les chemins.*"

Dating and Script: MH/LNS.

Remarks: Bo 9569 is a one-sided fragment whose lines 3′–5′ directly join Bo 9637:1′–3′ and KUB 15.33b IV 1′ (LNS). Bo 9569 + Bo 9637 + KUB 15.33b + IV 24–28 are parallel to KUB 15.34 IV 37′–42′ (MS), from were the restorations are taken. See also under: Bo 9637 + Bo 9569 + KUB 15.33b + ; Bo 9571 + KUB 15.38 + Bo 10125 +.

Measurements: 2.3 × 3.0 × 0.7 cm.

Bibliography: *Konkordanz,* http://www.hethport.uni-wuerzburg.de/hetskiz/sk.php?f=Bo%2069/264.

Bo 9569

Bo 9569 + Bo 9637 + rev. IV

Bo 9569 + Bo 9637 + KUB 15.33b + rev. IV (composite image)

Bo 9571 + Bo 10125 + Bo 9637 + Bo 9569 rev. IV

Reverse IV

(Line numbering follows KUB 15.38+; line numbers of Bo 9569 are in parentheses)

§ 3 24 (= 1′) I SILA$_4$[1)] *e-nu-um*[2)]*-mạ-aš-ši-i̯a* I <MUŠEN> *ḫa-r*[*i-i̯a*[3)] …*-zi-i̯a*[4)]] I UDU

25 (= 2′) *ḫa-az-zi-zi-i̯ạ*[5)] I MUŠEN *ú-nạ-x̣-*[…[6)] *k*]*i-iš-ḫi-i̯a*[7)] I UDU[8)]

26 (= 3′) [*z*]⌊*u-uz*⌋-[*zu-ma*]-⌊*k*⌋*i-i̯ạ kẹ-e*[*l-di-i̯a am-b*]⌈*a*?*-aš*?⌉-[*š*]*i u̯a-ar-nu-z*[*i*[9)]]

27 (= 4′) [*zé-e-a-an-ti-t*]*a QA-TAM-MA* ⌈*ir*⌉-[*ḫa-a-i*]⌈*z-zi*⌉[10)] *na-aš-tạ a-ra-aḫ-za*

28 (= 5′) [*aš-nu-ut-ta-at n*]*u* DINGIR.MEŠ MUNUS.MEŠ LUGA⌈L-*u*⌉*-iz-na-aš ŠA* KUR ^{URU}*Ḫa-at-ti*[11)] *šạ-r*[*a-a*]

…

(Bo 9569 breaks off here; the text after *ŠA* KUR ^{URU}*Ḫa-at-ti šạ-r*[*a-a*] continues in the following lines of Bo 9637 + KUB 15.33b)

Text-critical notes: [1)] KUB 15.34 IV 37′ omits I SILA$_4$. [2)] KUB 15.34 IV 37′: *e-nu-ma-*°. [3)] KUB 15.34 IV 37′: *ḫa-a-*°. [4)] Probably to *ḫu-u̯a-al-zi-i̯a*. [5)] KUB 15.34 IV 38′: I MUŠEN *ḫa-az-zi-iz-*°. [6)] Perhaps *ú-nạ-ạ*[*l-zi-i̯a*]; KUB 15.34 IV 38′ has *e-nu-ma-aš-ši-i̯a* instead. [7)] KUB 15.34 IV 39′ has *a-na-ni-iš-ḫi-i̯a* instead. [8)] KUB 15.34 IV 39′: I MUŠEN. [9)] KUB 15.34 IV 40′: *u̯a-ar-nu-an-zi*. [10)] KUB 15.34 IV 40′: *ir-ḫa-a-zi*. [11)] KUB 15.34 IV 41′ has DINGIR.MEŠ LÚ.MEŠ ^{GIŠ}ERIN-*aš* instead.

Bo 9570

Description: N/A.
CTH: 832 "*Fragments en langue hittite de nature inconnue*."
Dating and Script: LNS.
Remarks: One-sided and moderately abraded fragment.
Measurements: 3.5 × 2.7 × 0.9 cm.
Bibliography: N/A.

Bo 9570

§ 1′ 1′-2′ (traces)
3′]-*i̯-kán pa-ra-*⸢*a*?⸣(-)[[1]
4′]-*x̣-pa*?*-ši še-er* [
5′ *iš*?*-ḫ*]*u-u-u̯a-aš*[2] *x̣*(-)[
6′]-*x̣ i-da-l*[*u*?(-)
7′ (traces)
(broken off)

Text-critical notes: [1] Perhaps [*ḫa-aš-ši*]-*i̯-kán pa-ra-*⸢*a*⸣-[*iš*]; cf. FHG 2 + KUB 33.53 III 18′ (CTH 334.2.1.A): *na-at-ša-an ḫa-aš-ši-i̯* [… *pa-r*]*a-a-iš*. [2] Or to be restored as [*la-a*?*-ḫ*]*u-u-u̯a-aš* ? The alternative words [*išḫ*]*ūwaš* and [*lāḫ*]*ūwaš* "(s)he [po]ured on / over" are both very rare pret. sg. 3 forms and occur only in FHG 2 + KUB 33.53 III 20′, 24′ (Laroche, *Myth*. I, 81). These predicates and *idal*[*u*] "evi[l]" in the following line would fit a (magical) ritual with mythology.

Bo 9571 + KUB 15.38 + Bo 10125 +

Description: Evocation ritual.

CTH: 483.II.A *"Rituel: 'quand on tire les dieux sur les chemins.'"*

Dating and Script: MH/LNS.

Remarks: Bo 9571 is a one-sided fragment whose lines 1′–6′ directly join KUB 15.38 IV 21–26 (LNS) and Bo 10125:1′. Bo 9571 + KUB 15.38 + IV 21–26 are parallel to KUB 15.34 IV 35′–39′ (MS), from where the restorations are taken. See also under: Bo 9637 + Bo 9569 + KUB 15.33b + ; Bo 9569 + Bo 9637 + KUB 15.33b +

Measurements: 2.5 × 2.9 × 1.3 cm.

Bibliography: *Konkordanz,* http://www.hethport.uni-wuerzburg.de/hetskiz/sk.php?f=Bo%2069/264 (where Bo 9571 is mistakenly written Bo "9574").

Bo 9571

Bo 9571 + Bo 10125 + rev. IV

KUB 15.38 + Bo 9571 + Bo 10125 + rev. IV (composite image)

Bo 9571 + Bo 10125 + Bo 9637 + Bo 9569 rev. IV

Reverse IV

(Line numbering follows KUB 15.38+; line numbers of Bo 9571 are in parentheses)

§ 2 21 (= 1′) *u̯a-ar-nu-zi*[1] I [MUŠEN] *ḫ*⸢*u-u-u̯a*⸣-[*al-zi-i̯a ta-la-ḫu-ul-zi-i̯a*]

22 (= 2′) I MUŠEN-*ma ar-ḫa*(-)*x̣-x̣ u̯a-a*[*r-nu-zi*[2]]

---

§ 3 23 (= 3′) EGIR-*an-da-ma* DỊNGIR.M[E]Š MUNUS.MEŠ LUGAL-*u-i*[*z-na-aš ŠA* KUR ^{URU}*Ḫa-at-ti*[3])]

24 (= 4′) I SILA$_4$[4] *e-nu-um*[5]*-mạ-aš-ši-i̯a* I <MUŠEN> *ḫa-r*[*i-i̯a*[6] ...*-zi-i̯a*[7]] I UDU

25 (= 5′) *ḫa-az-zi-zi-i̯ạ*[8] I MUŠEN *ú-nạ-x̣*-[...[9]) *k*]*i-iš-ḫi-i̯a*[10] I UDU[11]

26 (= 6′) [*z*]⸤*u-uz*⸥-[*zu-ma*]-⸤*k*⸥*i-i̯ạ kẹ-e*[*l-di-i̯a am-b*]⸢*a*?*-aš*?⸣-[*š*]*i u̯a-ar-nu-z*[*i*[12]]

...

(Bo 9571 breaks off here; the text after *kẹ-e*[*l-di-i̯a* ...] continues in unpublished fragments Bo 10125 + Bo 9637 + Bo 9569)

Text-critical notes: 1) KUB 15.34 IV 35′: *u̯a-ar-nu-an-zi*. 2) Th. van den Hout suggests the reading *ar-ḫa-*[*i̯*]*a-ạn* (personal communication). KUB 15.34 IV 36′: I MUŠEN *ḫa-a-ri-i̯a u̯a-ar-nu-an-zi*. 3) Restoration follows KUB 60.151+ III 2′, Bo 9637+ IV 3′ and 6′, Bo 10125+ IV 3′ (all belong to the tablet KUB 15.38); KUB 15.34 IV 37′ has [DINGIR.ME]Š LÚ.MEŠ ^{GIŠ}ERIN-*aš* instead. 4) KUB 15.34 IV 37′ omits I SILA$_4$. 5) KUB 15.34 IV 37′: *e-nu-ma-*°. 6) KUB 15.34 IV 37′: *ḫa-a-*°. 7) Probably to *ḫu-u̯a-al-zi-i̯a*. 8) KUB 15.34 IV 38′: I MUŠEN *ḫa-az-zi-iz-*°. 9) Perhaps *ú-nạ-ạ*[*l-zi-i̯a*]; KUB 15.34 IV 38′ has *e-nu-ma-aš-ši-i̯a* instead. 10) KUB 15.34 IV 39′ has *a-na-ni-iš-ḫi-i̯a* instead. 11) KUB 15.34 IV 39′: I MUŠEN. 12) KUB 15.34 IV 40′: *u̯a-ar-nu-an-zi*.

Bo 9572

Description: N/A.

CTH: 832 "*Fragments en langue hittite de nature inconnue.*"

Dating and Script: NS.

Remarks: One-sided fragment that is too small to classify. Due to the narration in past tense, perhaps of historical nature.

Measurements: 3.3 × 2.2 × 1.5 cm.

Bibliography: N/A.

Bo 9572

§ 1′ 1′]-⌈*x̣*⌉
2′]-*x̣-nu-un* *x̣*$^{?}$[
3′](-)*ẹ*$^{?}$*-eš-ta*
4′ -*t*]*a*$^{?}$
(broken off)

Bo 9573

Description: Festival$^{?}$.

CTH: 670 "*Fragments divers.*"

Dating and Script: N/A. The script, however, appears to be older than NS.

Remarks: Tiny, one-sided fragment.

Measurements: 2.7 × 2.8 × 1.8 cm.

Bibliography: N/A.

Bo 9573

§ 1′	1′	](-)*a*$^{?}$-*x̣*-[
	2′	](-)*x̣*$^{?}$-*x̣* GAL(./-)⸢*x*⸣[
		————————
		————————
§ 2′	3′	-*z*]*i-uš-m*[*i*-[1)]
	4′	]-⸤*iz*$^{?}$-*z*⸥[*i*(-)
	(broken off)	

Text-critical note: [1)] The word structure suggests an adjective / noun + possessive pronoun, thus the restoration [*ḫa-an-te-ez-z*]*i-uš-m*[*i-iš*] "th[eir leade]rs" is tenable, although this usage appears elsewhere as *ḫa-an-te-ez-zi*(-*i̯a*)-*aš-mi-iš*; see KBo 20.32 III 13′, KUB 56.46 II 8′, KUB 59.19 II 7, etc. (all from Hattian cult milieu). On the other hand, J. Hazenbos reads (personal communication) [*ḫa-az-z*]*i-uš-m*[*i-it*] (*ḫazziu*=*šmit* "their cult provision"), which is comparable with *ḫa-az-ze-e-uš-še-et* (*ḫazzeu*=*šet*) in KUB 43.33 obv. 6 (OS).

Bo 9574

Description: Ritual or festival.

CTH: 470 "*Fragments de rituels*" or 670 "*Fragments divers.*"

Dating and Script: MS.

Remarks: One-sided fragment.

Measurements: 2.7 × 2.4 × 0.7 cm.

Bibliography: N/A.

Bo 9574

§ 1′	1′	(-)*u̯*]⸢*a*?-*ar*⸣-*x̣*(-)[
	2′	*šu-up-p*]*ị́*(?)-*i̯a-aḫ-ḫa-a*[*n*(-)
	3′	-*k*]*án-zi kị-ị*[*n*(?)-
	4′	] *ḫu-u-ma-an x̣*-[
§ 2′	5′	*a*]*r-ḫa* I?(-)*x̣*(-)[
	6′	(-)*d*]⸤*u-ni*(?)-*x*⸥(-)[

(broken off)

Bo 9575

Description: Ritual.

CTH: 401 "*Rituels analogues au précédent* (i.e., *Rituel d'Iriya, pour la purification d'une ville*)" or 421 "*Grand rituel de substitution*" ?

Dating and Script: pre-NS$^{?}$ or NS.

Remarks: One-sided fragment.

Measurements: 2.4 × 2.2 × 0.6 cm.

Bibliography: N/A.

Bo 9575

§ 1′ 1′]-⸢*x*(-)*im*$^{?}$ [1)]⸣- [
2′]-*mi-iš-n*[*a*$^{?}$(-)[2)]
3′] $^{Ẹ́}$*kip-pa*-⸢*a*⸣[*n*
4′]-*x̣-kán* ^{É}*ki*[*p-pa-*
5′ EGI]R-*pa tu-ụ-*[*u̯a*[3)]
6′]-⸤*x-š*⸥*a-i*(-)[
(broken off)

Text-critical notes: [1)] Or: ⸢NÍ⸣.[TE(./-)…]. [2)] Perhaps to be restored as [^{GIŠ}*kal*]-*mi-iš-n*[*a-*…] in connection with the burning of a ^{É}*kippa-*, which is a ritual act as seen in KUB 30.36 III 3′–4, 10′–12′ (CTH 401.1.A). [3)] For EGIR-*pa tūwa* in the same context mentioning ^{É}*kippa-*, see KUB 30.36 III 5′ and KUB 43.49 rev.$^{?}$ 38′ (CTH 421).

Bo 9576

Description: Oracle.

CTH: 582.

Dating and Script: NS.

Remarks: One-sided fragment from the lower-left portion of a tablet (with left edge and bottom part) that contains investigation(s) of cult negligences.

Measurements: 2.7 × 3.6 × 0.7 cm.

Bibliography: N/A.

Bo 9576

§ 1′ 1′ *ma-a-an ki-i-pá*[*t nam-ma-ma*[1]

---

§ 2′ 2′ *na-aš nam-ma pu-nu-u*[*š-šu-u*[?]*-e*[?]*-en nu me-mi-ir*[2]

3′ 𒑱[?]*ša*[3]*-kán-ta-at-tar*(-)[

4′ *ar-ḫa túḫ-š*⸤*a-an*[?]⸥(-)[… *nu-za* DINGIR-*LUM a-pád-da-an*[?]]

5′ *še-er* TUKU.TUKU-[*u-an-za*

(bottom of the tablet)

Text-critical notes: [1] Restoration follows KUB 16.16 obv. 12′, 22′, 31′, rev. 10, 17, 22, lt. e. 3 and KUB 18.20 obv.[?] 6. KUB 16.16 obv. 16′ has *nam-ma-i̯a* instead, whereas KUB 5.7 obv. 8, 28 and rev. 10, 17 use no *namma⸗*. [2] Cf. KUB 5.7 rev. 11, 14; KUB 16.16 obv. 13′, 17′, 23′, rev. 11, 18. Alternatively, KUB 18.14 III[?] 16′ has *UM-MA ŠU-NU-M*⸤*A*⸥. [3] It is not quite clear if a *glossenkeil*-word is present here since the scribe seems to have intended to write first a different sign than "*ša*." A plural form is also possible if one restores the word as *ša-kán-ta-at-tar-*[*ra*]. For *šakantattar* "appliqué[?]," see CHD Š/1 (2002) 40 f.; all occurrences listed there are without *glossenkeil* and not in a divination context.

Bo 9577

Description: Vow?.

CTH: 590 "*Fragments de songes et d'ex-voto.*"?

Dating and Script: NH/NS.

Remarks: One-sided fragment from the left column of a tablet, and its lines 2′–4′ may duplicate KUB 15.27 III 7′–9′ (CTH 590).

Measurements: 3.1 × 4.5 × 0.8 cm.

Bibliography: N/A.

Bo 9577

§ 1′ 1′ -*z*]*i-i*[*t*?

2′]-*x̣* *ḫal-zi-iḫ-ḫị-i̯a-a*⸢*t-t*⸣[*a*? [1)]]

3′ -*g*]*a*?-*nu-mi*[2)]

---

§ 2′ 4′ *še*]-*ḫi-li-iš-ki-aš*[3)] […?]

5′]-*x̣* *kẹ-e-*⸤*mu*?⸥[4)](-)[

(broken off)

Text-critical notes: [1)] I.e., *ḫalziḫḫi=ya=t*[*a*] "and I am calling yo[u]." [2)] Lines 2′–3′ strongly recall to mind the phrase [*ḫa*]*l-zi-iḫ-ḫi*(-)[…] / […]-*x̣-ga-nu-*[*mi*] in the vow text KUB 15.27 III 7′–8′, followed by a paragraph stroke in the next line like in Bo 9577. [3)] Although the cult term *šeḫiliški-* "purification ritual / offering" is chiefly proper to Kizzuwatnan rituals, line 4′ of our fragment containing this word and KUB 15.27 III 9′ can be combined as [*še-ḫi-li-iš-k*]*i-aš a-ri-i̯a-še-*⸢*eš-š*⸣[*ar*?] "oracle about (determination of) a purification ritual / offering." Thus, [*še*]*ḫiliškiaš* here is rather a sg. gen. form than pl. dat.-loc. [4)] Or, and less probably, *kẹ-e-ni*?*-x̣*?(-)[…].

Bo 9578

Description: N/A.

CTH: 832 "*Fragments en langue hittite de nature inconnue.*"

Dating and Script: NS.

Remarks: One-sided fragment that is too small to determine genre.

Measurements: 3.7 × 3.0 × 1.3 cm.

Bibliography: N/A.

Bo 9578

§ 1′	1′	]-*eš*?(-)*x̣*(-)[
	2′	.Ḫ]I.A(?) *x̣*-[
	3′	]-*i̯ạ* [
	4′	]-*x* *x̣*-[
§ 2′	5′	-*ḫ*]*a-lị-x̣*(-)[
	6′	]-*nạ*?-*x̣*(-)[
§ 3′	7′	]-*du-i̯a-kạ́n* *ḫụ*?-*x̣*-[
	8′	]-*x̣-an-da PA-NỊ A-ḪỊ*?-[
	9′	]-⌊x̣ LÚ.MEŠ⌋*ti-x̣*-[

(broken off)

Bo 9579

Description: Festival.

CTH: 670 "*Fragments divers.*"

Dating and Script: NS.

Remarks: Small, one-sided fragment.

Measurements: 2.8 × 2.7 × 0.7 cm.

Bibliography: N/A.

Bo 9579

§ 1′ 1′]⸢*x* *x*$^{?}$ *x*⸣

2′ ^{URU}*Ḫ*]*i-im-mu-u̯a*[1)]

3′] ^{LÚ}ALAM.Z[U$_9$]

4′ [*me-ma-i* ^{LÚ}*pal-u̯*]*a-tal-la-aš*

5′ [*pal-u̯a-a*$^{?}$*-iz-z*]*i*

(broken off)

Text-critical note: [1)] Most likely to be restored with [LÚ.MEŠ ^{URU}*Ḫ*]*i-im-mu-u̯a*; cf. KUB 7.11 obv. 1–7 (CTH 678.2) and its duplicate KBo 59.163 obv. 1′–3′.

Bo 9580

Description: Cult inventory or festival?.

CTH: 530 or 670 "*Fragments divers.*"?

Dating and Script: NS.

Remarks: One-sided fragment from the left column of a tablet. This fragment is reminiscent of the content of KBo 22.235, of which text category is not very certain (CTH 832; thus, according to the *Konkordanz*).

Measurements: 3.4 × 4.5 × 1.0 cm.

Bibliography: N/A.

Bo 9580

§ 1′ 1′]⌈*x x x*⌉[
2′] ⌈*i-i̯*⌉*a-at-ta* [

---

§ 2′ 3′ -*a*]*š*? *pa-a-an-zi*
4′](.)BURU$_{14}$[1)] *iš-tar-na ar-ḫ*[*a*]
5′]-*x̤ an-ni-iš-kán-zi*
6′ ^{L}]$^{Ú?}$*ṬE*$_4$*-ME i-i̯a-at-ta*
7′]-⌊*x*⌋-*zi* ^{KUŠ}*kur-šu-uš-u̯a*[2)]
8′]-⌊*x* ^{d}U⌋TU-*ŠI*
9′ (traces)
(broken off)

Text-critical notes: [1)]Further reading possibilities: [Ú].BAR$_8$ "[sp]ring," and [EZEN$_4$].BURU$_{14}$ or [EZEN$_4$ Ú].BAR$_8$ as a festival designation. [2)]Direct speech particle ≠*wa* here and ^{d}UTU-*ŠI* in the following line are striking features of the present context; for ^{d}UTU-*ŠI*, cf. also KBo 22.235 rev. 1′, which contains likewise the lexemes *ištarna arḫa* and *iyatta* (rev. 3′).

Bo 9581

Description: Ritual or festival.

CTH: 470 “*Fragments de rituels*” or 670 “*Fragments divers.*”

Dating and Script: NS.

Remarks: One-sided fragment.

Measurements: 3.7 × 3.3 × 1.4 cm.

Bibliography: N/A.

Bo 9581

§ 1′ 1′]-⸢*x-an*⸣(-)[
2′] LÀL?-*i̯*[*a*(-)
3′]-*x̣ ḫa-aš-š*[*i-i*?
4′ *I*]*Š-TU* GEŠ[TIN?
5′ *pé-eš-š*]*i-i̯a̯-az-z*[*i*
6′ -*i̯*]*a A-NA* GU[NNI
7′ BA]L-*an*- [*ti*]

---

§ 2′ 8′ U]ZUN⸤ÍG.GI⸥G.ḪI.Ạ(-)[
9′ (traces?)
(broken off)

Bo 9582

Description: Mythological.

CTH: 343.7 "*La royauté du dieu KAL.*"

Dating and Script: NS.

Remarks: One-sided fragment. Mention of the deity ^{d}LAMMA (lines 2′, 8′) in conjunction with the geographical names $^{\mathrm{ḪUR.SAG}}$Našalma (line 5′) and perhaps also *^{URU}Apzuwa (line 6′), secure the assignment of Bo 9582 to CTH 343. Its precise placement within the text composition, however, is not yet possible.

Measurements: 3.3 × 2.9 × 1.1 cm.

Bibliography: Soysal, *Anatolica* 38, 178 (transliteration and commentary).

Bo 9582

§ 1′ 1′ (traces)
2′ ^{d}L]AMMA *x̣*-[
3′ -*u*]*n*[1)] ẸZE⌜N$_4$-*an*⌝ [
4′]-*za*? *Ú-UL ku-u̯*[*a-pí-ik-ki*[2)]
5′ $^{\mathrm{ḪUR.S]ẠG}}$*Na-ša-al-m*[*a*(-)
6′ $^{\mathrm{UR]Ụ}}$*Ạp*(?)-*zụ-u-i-i̯*[*a*?(-)
7′]-*x̣*? *ụt-tar* ẸGIR-*an na*[*m*? [3)]-
8′] *Ạ-NA* ^{d}LAMM⌞A⌟ [
9′ (traces)
(broken off)

Text-critical notes: [1)] [*a-pu-u-u*]*n* or [*ku-u-u*]*n* ? [2)] For restoration, compare KUB 36.2d III 25′–26′ + KUB 33.112 III 19′. [3)] Or: *t*[*i-*…].

Bo 9583

Description: (Cult) inventory.

CTH: 250 "*Fragments d'inventaires*" or 530 "*Fragments divers.*"

Dating and Script: LNS.

Remarks: One-sided fragment including a portion of the left inscribed edge.

Measurements: 3.3 × 2.8 × 0.8 cm.

Bibliography: N/A.

Bo 9583

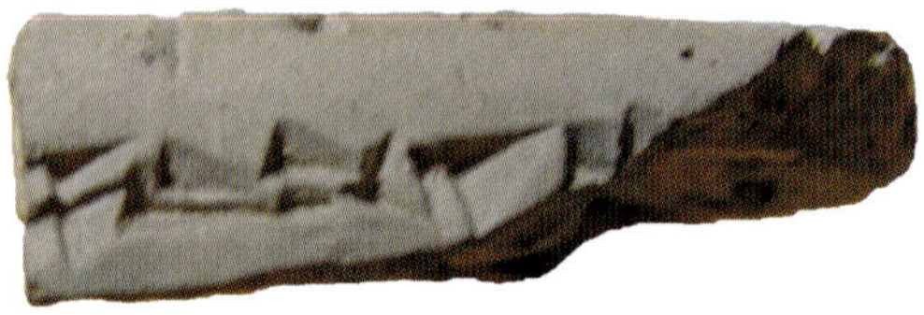

Bo 9583 (left edge)

§ 1′ 1′ ŠU.NÍGIN XXXVIII [

2′ ŠÀ VI *BI-IB-*[*RU*

3′ X *BI-IB-RU-m*[*a*

4′ ⸢VI$^{?}$⸣ ZA.LUM II *x̣*(./-)[

5′ [...](./-)*x̣* ŠÀ II BABBA[R$^{?}$

(broken off)

Left edge

1 -*z*]*a*$^{?1)}$-*ni-iš-x̣*-[

Text-critical note: [1)] Or: [...(-)*u*]*n-ni-iš-x̣*-[

Bo 9584

Description: Ritual$^{?}$.

CTH: 470 "*Fragments de rituels.*"

Dating and Script: NS.

Remarks: One-sided fragment from the right side (with edge) of a tablet. Possibly a ritual with participation of a reciting Old Woman.

Measurements: 3.9 × 2.5 × 1.4 cm.

Bibliography: N/A.

Bo 9584

Bo 9584 (right edge)

§ 1′ 1′]-⌈*x-ma*⌉

2′]-*x̣ ḫar-zi*

3′]-*ạ*$^{?}$*-aš-ša-u̯a-mu*

4′] *ụ́-e-ek-ti*

5′]-*x̣-ma-aš-ḫa* ŠÀ-*i*[*r*$^{?}$(-)…$^{?}$]

6′]-*ma-aš*

7′]-*ma* ^{MUNUS}ŠU.GI

8′]-*i̯ạ-u-u̯a-ar*

9′] *na-an nam-m*[*a*(-)…$^{?}$]

10′]-*za*$^{?}$ *ku-i*[*t*$^{?}$(-)

11′](-)⌊*x̣-š*⌋[*u*$^{?}$(-)

(broken off)

Bo 9585

Description: N/A.

CTH: 832 "*Fragments en langue hittite de nature inconnue.*"

Dating and Script: NS.

Remarks: One-sided fragment that cannot be determined (myth, ritual, or prayer?).

Measurements: 3.6 × 2.7 × 1.3 cm.

Bibliography: N/A.

Bo 9585

§ 1′ 1′]⸢*x-x*⸣[
2′](-)*ị-e-ez-z*[*i*
3′] *kị-ịt-tạ-r*[*i*
4′] *kạ-a-ša-u̯a a*[*n*?-[1)]
5′] *ạ-ru-e-eš-ki-ụ-*[*u̯a*?*-an*[2)]
6′](-)⸤*x̣*⸥*-nu*?*-an*[3)] *u̯a-a*[*l-ḫ̮i*?

---

§ 2′ 7′] ⸤*nu-z*⸥*a iš-x̣-*[[4)]
8′ (traces)
(broken off)

Text-critical notes: [1)] Or: As a divine name to be read ᵈ̣[…]. [2)] For this restored supine form to *aruwai-* "to bow, prostrate oneself" with a slight spelling variation, see *a-ru-ú-e-eš-ki-u-*[*u̯*]*a-an* in KUB 40.62 + KUB 13.9 I 5. [3)] The signs are not in favor of a reading [*m*]⸤*ar*⸥*-nu-an*. [4)] Read *iš-p*[*a-*…] or *iš-p*[*í-*…]; thus to *≈za išpai-/išpiya-* "to eat one's fill."

Bo 9586

Description: N/A.

CTH: 832 “*Fragments en langue hittite de nature inconnue*.”

Dating and Script: NS.

Remarks: One-sided fragment that is too small to determine.

Measurements: 2.5 × 3.2 × 0.6 cm.

Bibliography: N/A.

Bo 9586

§ 1′	1′	]⌈*x-x-x* ZABAR?⌉[
	2′	](-)*x̣*?-*a-i* [
	3′	]-*x̣*? *pa-ra-a pé-ẹ*?-[
	4′	] ⌊*ku-i*⌋*t* [
	5′	]-⌊*x-d*⌋[*u*?(-)
	(broken off)	

Bo 9587 + KUB 14.17

Description: Historical.

CTH: 61.II.4 "*Mursili II. Annales développées.*"

Dating and Script: Murš. II/LNS.

Remarks: Bo 9587 is a one-sided fragment whose lines 3′–9′ directly join KUB 14.17 III 1′–7′ (LNS).

Measurements: 2.9 × 3.2 × 0.6 cm.

Bibliography: Soysal, *Anatolica* 38, 172–73 (transliteration and translation).

Bo 9587

Bo 9587 + KUB 14.17 rev. III (composite image)

Reverse III

(Line numbers of Bo 9587 are in parentheses)

§ 1′ 1′ *A-NA*(?) ^{m}*An-n*]*i-i̯*⸢*a x-x*⸣(-)[…$^{?}$]

2′ *na*$^{?}$]*-an-za-an am-me-el*

3′ (= 1′) *-i*]⸢*š*$^{?}$ *x̣*$^{?}$⸣[ ]*-šu-un*

4′ (= 2′)]-⸢*t*⸣*a na-aš ú-i*[*t*] *nụ I-NA* ^{URU}*Da-an-ku-u̯a*

5′ (= 3′) [*i-i̯a-at-ta-at na-an* GU]L-*aḫ-ta na-an IŠ*-[*T*]*U* NAM.RA.MEŠ

6′ (= 4′) [GU$_4$ UDU *ša-ra-a da-a-aš na-an-kán I*]*-NA* ^{URU}*Ḫa-i̯a-ša ka*[*t-t*]*a-an-ta pé-e-dạ-aš*

---

§ 2′ 7′ (= 5′) [GIM-*an-ma-at* ^{d}UTU-*ŠI iš-ta-ma-aš-šu-un n*]*u-uš-ši ḫa-at-ra-a-nu-un zị-ik-u̯a-mu*

8′ (= 6′)] *ạ-pí-i̯a-u̯a-mu-kán Ú-UL kụ-ị-e-eš-ka*$_4$

x̣-[…*-i*]*r* LÚ.MEŠ ^{URU}*Ịš-te-te-na-i̯ạ-u̯ạ-mu-kán UL ku-i-e-eš-ka*$_4$ […$^{?}$]

9′ (= 7′) *zi-ik-ma-u̯a*] *ụ́-it nu-u̯a I-NA* KUR ^{URU}*Da-an-ku-u̯*[*a*]

(Bo 9587 breaks off here; text continues in KUB 14.17 III 8′)

Bo 9588

Description: Prayer (and ritual)$^?$.

CTH: 385 "*Fragments de prières à la déesse d'Arinna*$^?$."

Dating and Script: NH/LNS.

Remarks: One-sided fragment from the left side of a tablet.

Measurements: 3.0 × 2.8 × 1.0 cm.

Bibliography: N/A.

Bo 9588

§ 1′ 1′ [^{L}]⌈$^{Ú.MEŠ}$*ḫa-x*⌉-[
2′ *ạr-ša-* [

---

§ 2′ 3′ ^{LÚ}*tu-uḫ-kán-ti-i̯[a*$^?$-
4′ *ŠA* DINGIR-*LIM* ^{GIŠ}*ši-i̯[a*$^?$- …[1])]
5′ IGI-*an-da e-e[p-zi*
6′ *an-da me-ma-[i*

---

§ 3′ 7′ ^{d}UTU ^{URU}PÚ-*na* GAŠAN-*Y[A*[2])
8′ *nu-u̯a šạ*$^?$*-i-x̣-*[
9′ ⌊*nu-u̯*⌋*a x*-⌊*x*⌋(-)[
(broken off)

Text-critical notes: [1]) Following the name of the goddess mentioned in line 7′, a restoration [… *A-NA* ^{d}UTU ^{URU}PÚ-*na*] would be expected here. [2]) Although the expression "O Sun-goddess of Arinna, m[y] Lady," as part of the recitation addressed to the deity, would suggest a prayer or vow for the text genre of Bo 9588, the scenery in lines 4′–6′ fits rather a ceremony in a ritual or festival.

Bo 9589

Description: Cult inventory.

CTH: 530 *"Fragments divers."*

Dating and Script: NH/LNS.

Remarks: One-sided fragment.

Measurements: 4.2 × 2.6 × 0.8 cm.

Bibliography: N/A.

Bo 9589

§ 1′ 1′ (traces)

2′ -*k*]*án* *ANA* DINGI[R(./-)[1]

3′ *ḫu-e-šu-u*?]-*u̯a-za* *z*[*é-i̯a*?-*an-ta-za*

4′ ^{DUG}*ḫa-ni-iš-ša-aš*] KAŠ *IŠ-TU* É̩-[*ŠU pé-e-da-i*(?)[2]

5′ *BI*]-*I̩B-RI*$^{\text{ḪI.A}}$-*kán* [...? *šu-un-na-an-zi*(?)[3]

6′ GAL.ḪI.A-*kán a*]*š-ša-nu-u̯a-an-z*[*i* ...?]

---

§ 2′ 7′] *pí-i̯a-an-z*[*i*

8′] *ša-ra-a d*[*a-an-zi*

9′] I UDU *š*⌊*a-x̣*⌋-[

(broken off)

Text-critical notes: [1] Or to be read as a divine name ^{d}[...]. [2] As the agent of the sentence, a priest is expected here; see KUB 25.23 I 5′ and ibid., lt. e. (left half) lines 2–3, from where the restorations for Bo 9589:4′ are taken. [3] Alternatively, to be restored with the verbal form *šu*(-*u*)-*u̯a-an-zi*; cf. KUB 25.23 I 20′, 30′, 46′, KUB 44.1 rev. 11′, etc.

Bo 9590

Description: Ritual or festival.

CTH: 470 "*Fragments de rituels*" or 670 "*Fragments divers.*"

Dating and Script: NS.

Remarks: Tiny, one-sided fragment.

Measurements: 2.9 × 3.6 × 0.9 cm.

Bibliography: N/A.

Bo 9590

§ 1′ 1′]-⸢*iz*?⸣-*z*[*i*(-)

2′]-⸢*š*⸣*a-ra-a*[*n*(-)[1]

3′ L]IBIR?-*RI* x̣(-)[

4′] ⸢SÍG⸣*ki-i*[*š-ri*?-

---

§ 2′ 5′ SÍG?*k*]*i*?-*iš-r*⸤*i*?⸥-[

6′]⸤*x-x*⸥[

(broken off)

Text-critical note: [1] Possibly belongs to the noun SÍG*a/ešara-* "wool string."

Bo 9591

Description: N/A.

CTH: 832 "*Fragments en langue hittite de nature inconnue.*"

Dating and Script: NS.

Remarks: One-sided fragment that is too small to classify.

Measurements: 3.3 × 1.6 × 2.0 cm.

Bibliography: N/A.

Bo 9591

§	Line	Text
§ 1′	1′	(-)*š*]*a*?(-)[
	2′	] *x̣*-[
§ 2′	3′	]-*a*?-*an* [
	4′	]-*x̣*-*na*-*a*[*n*(-)
	5′	-*ḫ*]*u*-*ụn*-*d*[*a*-[1]
	6′	D]AM?-*ŠU*(-)[
	7′	E]ME-*an* [
	8′	](-) *x̣*-*x̣*?(-)[

(broken off)

Text-critical note: [1] A Hittite word (participle) or proper name including the divine element Tarḫunda- ?

Bo 9593

Description: Luwian.

CTH: 770 "*Fragments en langue louvite.*"

Dating and Script: NS.

Remarks: One-sided fragment. Although there is no complete word in this fragment, the non-Hittite language here seems to bear a closer resemblance to Luwian.

Measurements: 2.8 × 3.1 × 0.6 cm.

Bibliography: N/A.

Bo 9593

§ 1′ 1′]-⌈*x̣* $^{L⌉Ú}$SI[PA(?)

---

§ 2′ 2′ *i*]⌈*š*?-*ḫ*⌉*i-i̯a-an-du x̣*?(eras.) GÍ[R(./-)[1]

3′](-)*ku-u̯a-ap-na-an-ti*[2]*-ká*[*n*

4′ -*t*]*i-kán*[2] *iš-ti*[3]*-na-aš-š*[*i*(-)

5′]⌊*x-x-x*⌋ *u̯a-ra-a*[*n*-

6′](-)⌊*a*?⌋-*r*[*a*-

7′](-)*x̣-x̣*(-)[

8′ (traces)

(broken off)

Text-critical notes: [1] This line seems to be written (partially) in Hittite. For the logogram GÍR "knife," which occurs in Luwian(-Hittite) context, see, e.g., KUB 35.143 II 5′ and KUB 44.4+ rev. 4 (Starke, StBoT 30, 229, 234). [2] To be restored with the word in the previous line? [3] The remarkable shape of the sign "*ti*" is reminiscent of those in KUB 35.68:4′, 11′, 12′. It should furthermore be noticed that Bo 9593 and KUB 35.68 (NS) exhibit very similar ductus.

Bo 9594

Description: Ritual or festival.

CTH: 470 "*Fragments de rituels*" or 670 "*Fragments divers.*"

Dating and Script: NS.

Remarks: One-sided fragment.

Measurements: 2.8 × 2.0 × 1.1 cm.

Bibliography: N/A.

Bo 9594

§ 1′	1′	](-)⌈*x̣*$^{?}$-*š*⌉*a*-*x̣*(-)[
	2′	](-)*x̣*-*az*(-)[
	3′	](-)*x̣*-*an*-*ku*-*x̣*(-)[
	4′	] *ki*-*it*-*t*[*a*(-)
	5′	]-*x̣*-*na*-*al*-*l*[*i*(-)$^{1)}$
§ 2′	6′	-*u̯*]*a*$^{?}$-*aš*$^{!?\ 2)}$-*ša*-*a*[*n*-
	7′	(traces)
	(broken off)	

Text-critical notes: $^{1)}$ To be restored as [^{DUG}*pa-aḫ-ḫ*]*u-na-al-l*[*i*(-)…] or better [^{MUNUS}*ḫu-u̯a-aš-ša-a*]*n-na-al-l*[*i*(-)…]? $^{2)}$ This sign shows an unusual shape, possibly first intended to be written "*ša*" although no erasure is seen here. Thus, the readings [^{MUNUS}*ḫu-u̯*]*a-aš*$^{!?}$-*ša-a*[*n-na-al-li*(-)…] and [^{d}*Ḫu-u̯*]*a-aš*$^{!?}$-*ša-a*[*n-na*(-)…] are conceivable; cf. KBo 29.65+ IV 3′–4′ and KBo 24.22:13′–14′. If the female profession ^{MUNUS}*ḫuwaššannalla/i-* is present in lines 5′–6′, the text can be assigned to CTH 692–94.

Bo 9595

Description: Treaty.

CTH: 139 *"Traité passé avec les Gasgas."*

Dating and Script: MH/MS.

Remarks: One-sided fragment. Due to the remarkable sign forms and archaic ligature writings "*kat+ta*, *kat+ti*, ME+EŠ," Bo 9595 may not belong to the same tablet as KUB 31.104(+)KBo 16.29 (pace *Konkordanz*).

Measurements: 1.8 × 2.6 × 0.8 cm.

Bibliography: *Konkordanz,* http://www.hethport.uni-wuerzburg.de/hetskiz/sk.php?f=10/a.

Bo 9595

§ 1′ 1′]-⌈*kán*⌉(-)[1] [

---

§ 2′ 2′ [m... m... ... L]Ú.MEŠ *kat+ti-iš-mi* U[RU?... *nu-za li-in-ki-i̯a*]

3′ [*ták-šu-la-aš ut-tar kat-ta-an QA-TAM-MA-pát da-i*]-*ẹ-er* (eras.)[2]

ÉRIN.ME.EŠ-*az kat+t*[*a-an*[3] *da-i-e-er*[4]]

(broken off)

Text-critical notes: [1] Perhaps [*az-zi-ik*]-⌈*kán*⌉-[*du*]; cf. KBo 8.35 II 24′. [2] Seemingly, a number is erased here. [3] The very same ligature writing is attested in KBo 58.270:3′ where one reads [ÉRIN.M]E.EŠ-*az kat+ta-an*. Considering the ductus, tablet features, and frequent erasures, I suspect that KBo 58.270 and Bo 9595 belong to the same tablet. [4] Restorations for lines 2′–3′ are taken from KBo 8.35 II 30′–31′; cf. also KBo 16.29(+) I? 12′–20′.

Bo 9596

Description: N/A.

CTH: 832 "*Fragments en langue hittite de nature inconnue.*"

Dating and Script: NS.

Remarks: One-sided fragment (including a part of the right edge) that is too small to determine.

Measurements: 4.3 × 1.9 × 1.7 cm.

Bibliography: N/A.

Bo 9596

Bo 9596 (right edge)

§ 1′ 1′ *-l*]*i* [

2′]-*x̣-šạ-ạn*

3′]-*e*

4′]-*x̣-te-ni*

---

§ 2′ 5′ *-d*]*a-ni*

6′] *nẹ-pị́-š*[*a-*

7′]-⌊*a*⌋*ḫ̣*$^?$-⌊*ḫu*⌋-[*u*]⌊*n*$^?$⌋

(broken off)

Bo 9597

Description: N/A.

CTH: 832 “*Fragments en langue hittite de nature inconnue.*”

Dating and Script: NS.

Remarks: One-sided fragment from the bottom part of a tablet that is too small to classify.

Measurements: 3.2 × 2.3 × 1.1 cm.

Bibliography: N/A.

Bo 9597

§ 1′ 1′]-*ku*$^{?}$(-)[

2′$^{?}$ …

3″ *ḫ*]*a*$^{?}$*-tu-ki*[1)] [

4″] I-*e-da-*[*ni*

5″ *i*]*š-ḫu-u-u̯a-a-*[*i*$^{?}$

6″ $^{GIŠ?}$*in-t*]*a-lu-uz-z*[*i*(-)

(bottom of the tablet)

Text-critical note: [1)] If the reading posed here is correct, the word may be a dat.-loc. form of *ḫatuka-* “terrifying,” which appears also in some ritual contexts mentioning *išḫuwai-* “to pour, scatter” in KBo 17.105+ III 6–9 and $^{(GIŠ)}$*intaluzzi-* “shovel” in KBo 12.111:1′–5′.

Bo 9598

Description: Cult of Nerik.

CTH: 678.3.F "*Fragments de fêtes diverses.*"

Dating and Script: NH/LNS.

Remarks: One-sided fragment with a part of the right edge. Bo 9598 lines 1′–7′ are duplicate or parallel to Bo 3315 + obv. 4′–9′ (CTH 678.3.A) and KUB 55.60 + III$^{?}$ 1′–7′ (CTH 678.3.B) from where the restorations are taken. Whether lines 1′–7′ of Bo 9598 indirectly join KUB 55.60 + III$^{?}$ 1′–7′ seems to be unlikely, since the handwriting on the tablets is not identical. Moreover, Bo 9598 has a double paragraph stroke before line 1′; in KUB 55.60 + the paragraph stroke is single.

Measurements: 2.7 × 2.9 × 0.4 cm.

Bibliography: Haas, *KN*, 277a (to Bo 3315 +); Fuscagni, HPMM 6, 24 (to Bo 3315 +).

Bo 9598

Obverse II$^{?}$ (or reverse III$^{?}$)

§ 1′ …

——

——

§ 2′ 1′] *Ạ*$^{?}$*-NA* DINGIR.MEŠ *da-p*⸢*í*⸣*-*[*aš*]

2′]*-x̣ ŠA* ^{d}U ^{URU}*N*[*e-ri-ik-ka*$_4$]

3′ *-i̯*]*a*$^{?}$*-kán* ^{DUG}*ḫar-ši-i̯*[*a-al-li*]

4′]⸤NINDA⸥.GUR$_4$.RA 1 ^{DUG}*KU-KU-*[*UB* …$^{?}$]

5′]*-x̣ ma-la-an-z*[*i*]

6′]*-x̣*[1)]

---

§ 3′ 7′ *-a*]⸤*n*$^{?}$*-zi*[2)]⸥

(broken off)

Text-critical notes: [1)] After KUB 55.60 + III$^{?}$ 6 and Bo 3315 + obv. 8′ this line is to be restored as [ZÌ.DA.A DÙ*-an-zi* GE$_6$*-ti-ma-at ḫar-ra-an-z*]*i*. However, KUB 55.60 + III$^{?}$ 6 alternatively has *i̯š-pa-a*[*n-ti-ma-at*]. [2)] Following Bo 3315 + obv. 9′ this line is expected to read [EZEN$_4$ *DI*$_{12}$*-ŠI* DÙ*-a*]⸤*n-zi*⸥.

Bo 9599 + KUB 58.94

Description: Ritual.

CTH: 395 *"Rituel de Hantitassu: 'si les années d'un homme sont gâtées.'"*

Dating and Script: MH/NS.

Remarks: Bo 9599 is a one-sided fragment whose lines 1′–6′ directly join KUB 58.94 I 8′–13′ (NS).

Measurements: 2.2 × 2.6 × 0.7 cm.

Bibliography: N/A.

Bo 9599

KUB 58.94 + Bo 9599 obv. I (detail)

KUB 58.94 + Bo 9599 obv. I

Obverse I

(Line numbers of Bo 9599 are in parentheses)

§ 2′ 8′ (= 1′) *nu-u̯a-za da-pí-an-du-uš* DINGIR.MEŠ-*uš ḫal-zi-iḫ-ḫu-u̯*[*n*$^{?}$ [1)]

9′ (= 2′) *nu-u̯a-za da-pí-an-du-uš* DUMU.MEŠ.LÚ.Ụ$_{19}$.LỤ *ḫal-zi-i*[*ḫ-ḫu-un* EN.SISKUR-*ma*[2)]]

10′ (= 3′) *me-er-ta-at nu-u̯a-ra-an-za-an Ụ́-UL ḫal-zi-i*[*ḫ-ḫu-un* …$^{?}$ DINGIR.MEŠ …$^{?}$ [3)]]

11′ (= 4′) *pa-ra-a ti-i-e-er nu* ^{d}UTU-*i me-mi-ir ki-nu-u*[*n*(-)[4)]

12′ (= 5′) *nu-u̯a-ra-an-za-an UL ḫal-z*[*i-i̯*]*a-u-e-ni UM-MA* ḍ[UTU

13′ (= 6′) *nu-u̯a-kán ku-it a-a*[*š*$^{?}$-[5)] …]⌊*x x x x x x*⌋[

(Bo 9599 breaks off here; text continues in KUB 58.94 I 14′ ff.)

Text-critical notes: [1)] After this direct join, the new readings for lines 8′–13′ necessitate some corrections to the transliteration made by Ünal, *Ḫantitaššu*, 95. [2)] For restoration, see Ünal, ibid., 95 n. 58 (with reference to KUB 57.79 I 12′). [3)] It is not clear if there is enough space for an additional *da-pí-an-du-uš*; see, e.g., KUB 58.94 I 14′, where only DINGIR.MEŠ is written. [4)] Cf. also KUB 57.79 I 14′. [5)] Ünal, ibid., 95, reads *A-N*[*A*].

Bo 9601

Description: N/A.

CTH: 832 “*Fragments en langue hittite de nature inconnue.*”

Dating and Script: NS.

Remarks: One-sided fragment that cannot be identified.

Measurements: 3.0 × 2.9 × 0.8 cm.

Bibliography: N/A.

Bo 9601

§ 1′ 1′](-)*x̣-x̣*(-)[

2′]-*x̣-nạ*?-*aš* IGI.Ḫ⸢I.A⸣(-)[

3′ -*u̯*]*a*?-*an-za e-eš-t*[*a*?

4′ *a-pí*(?)-*n*]*i-eš-šu-u̯a-an*[1)] *x̣*-[

5′]-*x̣* EGIR-*pa me-mi-i*[*š*-[2)]

6′](-)⸤*x*⸥-[…?]-*la-a-i x̣*-[

7′](-)⸤*x̣*?-*x̣-x*⸥(-)[

(broken off)

Text-critical notes: [1)] Or [*ka-n*]*i-eš-šu-u̯a-an* ? [2)] Possibly to be restored as *me-mi-i*[*š-ki-iz-zi*] or *me-mi-i*[*š-ki-u*?-*u̯a-an da-a-iš*]. The phrase EGIR-*pa mema-* “to reply” in the beginning of a new paragraph would suggest that the fragment in question belongs to a mythological composition.

Bo 9602 (+[?]) KUB 39.61

Description: Ritual or festival.

CTH: 470 "*Fragments de rituels*" or 670 "*Fragments divers*."

Dating and Script: LNS (or a bit "careless script.")

Remarks: One-sided fragment that contains a partial colophon. Bo 9602 can be tentatively suggested as part of KUB 39.61 IV (colophon; CTH 470.93), which exhibits in lines 1′–2′ likewise more careless script than in the main text. Both fragments are deposited in different locations so that a physical examination to determine whether they belong to the same tablet is not possible.

Measurements: 2.6 × 3.7 × 1.2 cm.

Bibliography: N/A.

Bo 9602

Colophon

§ 1′ 1′] DỤB.I.KẠM *QA*-⌈*TI*⌉ [

2′ LUG]AL-*uš* *pu-u-ri-i*[*n*[1]

3′ *n*]*u* SISKUR[2] GIM-*a*[*n*(-)[3]

(broken off)

Text-critical notes: [1] Although *pu-u-ri-in* "lip, rim" (acc.) employs mostly the acts *dāi-* "to set, put" and *zikk-* "to place" (CHD P/3 [1997] 385), the verb *epp-* "to take" could probably come into consideration as well, e.g., in: *nu-uš-ši-kán* LUGAL-*uš*-⌈*za*!⌉(eras.) *pu-u-ri-in* / [DI]B[?]-*zi* in KUB 39.61 I 3–4 (following Mouton, *Rêves*, 152). [2] SISKUR "ritual" may indicate that this is more likely a ritual text, and not a festival description. [3] If one attempts to detect an indirect join between Bo 9602:3′ and KUB 39.61 IV 2′ then this line reads: [*n*]*u* SISKUR GIM-*a*[*n* …[?]] *i-i̯a-an-z*⌈*i*⌉.

Bo 9603

Description: N/A.

CTH: 832 "*Fragments en langue hittite de nature inconnue.*"

Dating and Script: N/A.

Remarks: Two-sided fragment from the upper and lower edge portions of a tablet; too small to classify.

Measurements: 2.0 × 4.2 × 1.7 cm.

Bibliography: N/A.

Bo 9603 obv.?

Bo 9603 rev.?

Obverse?

§ 1	1	](.)* x̣*?.SAG[1)] *x̣*(-/.)[
	2	]-⌊*x*-*x*?⌋-*x̣* [
	3	]⌊*x*-*x*-*x*-*x*?-*x*⌋[
	(broken off)	

Reverse?

§ 1′	1′	](-)⌈*x̣*(-)*ša-mu*?⌉(-)[
	(bottom of the tablet)	

Text-critical note: [1)] If the word UR.SAG "hero" is present here, this line could be part of the genealogy of a Hittite king.

Bo 9604

Description: Festival.

CTH: 670 "*Fragments divers.*"

Dating and Script: NS.

Remarks: One-sided fragment from the bottom part of a tablet.

Measurements: 2.3 × 3.3 × 0.7 cm.

Bibliography: N/A.

Bo 9604

§ 1′ 1′](-)⌈*x-x*⌉(-)[

2′](-)⌈*x̣*⌉-*u̯š* ⌈*ti*?-*an-zi*⌉[1)][

---

§ 2′ 3′ G]UB?-*aš* II NINDA.GUR$_4$.R[A.ḪI.A *pár-ši-i̯a*(?)[2)]

(bottom of the tablet)

Text-critical notes: [1)] Or: ⌈BAL-*an-zi*⌉. [2)] For the rare offering act of "breaking breads in standing position," see KUB 27.1 I 47: I NINDA.SIG dU-*up* GUB-*aš pár-ši-i̯a*.

Bo 9605 + Bo 3396 + KBo 53.308

Description: Oracle.

CTH: 574.21 "*Oracles par l'oiseau Ḫurri.*"

Dating and Script: NS.

Remarks: Bo 9605 is a one-sided fragment whose lines 2′–6′ directly join unpublished fragment Bo 3396 I$^?$ 2′–6′ and KBo 53.308:1′–2′. Further, Bo 3396 IV$^?$ 4′–8′ directly join KBo 52.102, which is not included here.

Measurements: 3.0 × 3.4 × 1.3 cm.

Bibliography: KBo 52, *Inhaltsverzeichnis*, p. VII (to KBo 52.102 + Bo 3396 IV$^?$); Soysal, *JAOS* 129, 306 (to KBo 53.308); *Konkordanz,* http://www.hethport.uni-wuerzburg.de/hetskiz/sk.php?f=1096/u.

Bo 9605

Bo 3396 + Bo 9605 + KBo 53.308 obv. I$^?$

Obverse I?

(Line numbers of Bo 9605 are in parentheses)

§ 1′ 1′ (= 1′) IV? [1](-)*x*(-)[...] [

---

§ 2′ 2′ (= 2′) *ụa-aš-ku-uš ŠA* É.NA$_4$ DINGI[R-*LIM*[2]

3′ (= 3′) *ŠA* EZEN$_4$*da-ḫi-ia-aš ḫar-ra-a*[*n*(-)

4′ (= 4′) IGI.DU$_8$.A *kar-aš-*[*š*]*a-an ḫal-ku*!*-ụ́*? [3]-[

5′ (= 5′) GA *ḫu-u-el-pí kụ-i*⌊*t pé*⌋*-ẹš-*⌈*kir*⌉ *na-*[*at*(-)

6′ (= 6′) *ḫa-aš-pé-el-lạ*[4] *k*[*a*]*r-aš-ša-an x*-[

(Bo 9605 breaks here off; text continues in Bo 3396 I? 7′–10′ and KBo 53:308:3′–4′)

7′ *kạr-aš-ša-an-za ḫal-k*⌊*u-ú-i*⌋*-eš-šar-ra k*[*u-it*]

8′ *pé-e ḫar-kir n*[*a-at*(-) ...](-)⌊x-x⌋[

9′ *nụ* GIŠ.^{d}INANNA *ka*[*r-aš-ša-an*(-)

10′ UDU ḪA.LA-*ia x*[5]-[

(obv. I? breaks off here; rev. IV? is in KBo 52.102 + Bo 3396)

Text-critical notes: [1] Alternatively read "GAR, NÍG" or "NINDA"; cf. NINDA KAŠ in KBo 54.113:2′. [2] For the phrase "the failures concerning the divine stone house (i.e., mausoleum)," see KUB 18.32:6′, 13′, KBo 54.113:(1′), and KBo 55.199:5′, which are, according to the *Konkordanz*, fragments of the same tablet. [3] Seemingly, the second sign "*ku*!" was first written as "*ki*," and the word can also be read *ḫal-ku*!*-ẹ-*[...]. In any case, and without doubt, the incomplete word goes back to *ḫalkueššar* "(cultic) supplies" and occurs again in line 7′. [4] *ḫa-aš-pé-el-la* (perhaps to be analyzed as *ḫašpel=a*) is a hapax of unknown meaning. If it is a Hittite word one poses a formation *ḫašp-* "to destroy" with nominal ending *-el*, in the sense of "destruction" or something similar. On the other hand, it could be a special (cult) designation borrowed from Hattian. A possible nominal stem **ḫašpil* in this language would be considered a masculine form to *ḫa-a-aš-pí-ú* as it occurs in Hattian context KUB 48.47 rt. col. 4′ (Soysal, *HWHT*, 454); for similar nominal formations in Hattian, see, e.g., ^{d}*Ḫašamil* < ^{d}*Ḫašmaiu* and *ḫāštaēl* < *ḫāštau* (Soysal, *HWHT*, 145, 455). [5] Possibly *k*[*ar-aš-ša-an-za*]; cf. KBo 55.199:3′.

Bo 9606

Description: Ritual or festival.

CTH: 470 "*Fragments de rituels*" or 670 "*Fragments divers.*"

Dating and Script: N/A.

Remarks: Small, one-sided tablet fragment including a portion of the partially inscribed right edge.

Measurements: 4.3 × 1.0 × 2.2 cm.

Bibliography: N/A.

Bo 9606

Bo 9606 (right edge)

§ 1′ 1′ …

______

§ 2′ 2′ UG]ULA$^{?}$ LÚ$^{?}$.[

3′ *I-N*]*A*(?) ỤD.IỊ.⸢KAM(?)-*i̯a-x*⸣(-)[

4′ I]GI-*zi* UD-*ti* [...$^{?}$]

5′ -*n*]*a-an-zị*

______

______

§ 3′ 6′]-*x̣-aḫ*$^{?}$-*zị*

7′]-*x̣*

8′](-)*x̣*(-)[...$^{?}$] ỤDU$^{?}$(./-)*x̣*-[...$^{?}$]-*x̣*

9′ (illegible signs)

10′ (illegible signs) On the other side is seen: [...]-⸢*i̯a*⸣

(broken off)

Bo 9607

Description: N/A.

CTH: 832 "*Fragments en langue hittite de nature inconnue.*"

Dating and Script: N/A.

Remarks: One-sided fragment that cannot be identified.

Measurements: 3.3 × 3.1 × 1.2 cm.

Bibliography: N/A.

Bo 9607

§ 1′ 1′]-*x̣*$^{?}$ ⸢*ma*$^{?}$-*a-an*$^{?}$⸣(-)[
2′ -*š*]*a-aš-ma-aš k*⸢*i*⸣-[
3′ …

---

§ 2′ 4′ *n*]*a*$^{?}$-*a-u-i*[1)] *n*[*a*$^{?}$-
5′ (-)*t*]*a*$^{?}$-*ga-a*[*n*(-)
6′]-*x̣ nu*(-)[
7′ (traces$^{?}$)
(broken off)

Text-critical note: [1)] It is doubtful whether the word *nāwi* "not yet" is present here since it is always spelled with "*ú*." The only exception, *na-a-u-i*(-)*x*(-)[…] in KBo 53.171:6′, is not certain either. Another possibility would be the reading [*ḫar-n*]*a-a-u-i* "on the [birth] stool" (J. Hazenbos, personal communication); cf. the form *ḫar-na-u-*[*i*] in ABoT 17+ III 6′.

Bo 9608

Description: N/A.

CTH: 832 *"Fragments en langue hittite de nature inconnue."*

Dating and Script: N/A.

Remarks: One-sided fragment that is not to be determined.

Measurements: 3.3 × 3.9 × 1.0 cm.

Bibliography: N/A.

Bo 9608

Left column

§ 1′ 1′ -*z*]⸢*i*?⸣

---

§ 2′ 2′ …

3′ -*i̥*]*a*?

4′ -*a*]*n-zi*

5′]-*x̥*

(broken off)

Right column

§ 1′ 1′ …

---

§ 2′ 2′ I [

3′ *a*⸤*n*⸥[1)]-[

(broken off)

Text-critical note: [1)] Or: DINGI⸤R⸥.

Bo 9609

Description: N/A.

CTH: 832 "*Fragments en langue hittite de nature inconnue*."

Dating and Script: NS.

Remarks: One-sided fragment that cannot be identified.

Measurements: 3.3 × 1.8 × 1.0 cm.

Bibliography: N/A.

Bo 9609

§ 1′ 1′]-*x̣*$^{?}$-*it m*[*a*-
2′]-*x̣ zi*-*x̣*(-)[

---

§ 2′ 3′ -*a*]*n*$^{?}$ *x̣*-*x̣*(-)[
4′ (-)*š*]*a*-*an* [
5′]-*x̣*-*i ak*-*x̤* -[
6′](-)*x̣*$^{?}$-*a*-*ši nu*-*m*[*u*(-)

---

§ 3′ 7′](-)*l*⌊*i*-*x*⌋(-)[
(broken off)

Bo 9610

Description: Ritual or festival.

CTH: 470 "*Fragments de rituels*" or 670 "*Fragments divers.*"

Dating and Script: NS.

Remarks: Small, one-sided fragment.

Measurements: 3.5 × 2.4 × 1.4 cm.

Bibliography: N/A.

Bo 9610

§ 1′ 1′]-*x̣*? É̩.⸢DINGIR-*LI*⸣[*M*?
2′ -*u*]*š* [
3′ …
4′ DI]M_4 BAPPI⸤R⸥[
5′]-*x̣* *ŠA* LÚ *x̣*?[
6′]-*ạ*?-*u̯a-kán* [
7′]-*x̣* *za-nu-*⸤*u̯*⸥[*a-*
8′ (traces)
(broken off)

Bo 9611

Description: Ritual or festival.

CTH: 470 "*Fragments de rituels*" or 670 "*Fragments divers*."

Dating and Script: NS.

Remarks: Small, one-sided fragment.

Measurements: 2.9 × 2.0 × 1.2 cm.

Bibliography: N/A.

Bo 9611

§ 1′ 1′]*x̣-x̣*[

2′ *ki-iš-ša-a*]*n*(?) *ḫ*⌈*u-x̣*⌉-[[1)]

---

§ 2′ 3′]-*ẹ*[?]-*mu-u-ur-x̣*(-)[

4′](-)⌊*x̣*[?]-*iš*⌋-*šu* *x̣*-[

5′]-*x̣* *t*[*a*-

6′ (traces[?])

(broken off)

Text-critical note: [1)] Possibly belongs to the verb *ḫu*(*e*)*k*- "to conjure." The following lines (2′–5′) are in a non-Hittite language.

Bo 9612

Description: Ritual.

CTH: 409 *"Rituel de Tunnawiya, contre l'impureté."*?

Dating and Script: NS.

Remarks: One-sided fragment that is from the left column (obv. I?) of a tablet. Bo 9612 may most likely belong to the Tunnawiya ritual; its precise placement within the text composition (and its versions), however, is not possible.

Measurements: 1.9 × 4.0 × 1.2 cm.

Bibliography: N/A.

Bo 9612 obv. I?

Obverse I?

§ 1′ 1′] ⸢I *UP-NU* DIM$_4$[1)] I *UP-NỤ*?⸣[2)]

2′ I] *UP-NU* *pár-ḫu-i-na-aš*

3′ …

---

§ 2′ 4′] ⸤^{NINDA}*ma-ri*⸥-*i*-⸤*e-eš*⸥[3)]

(broken off)

Text-critical notes: [1)] According to the traces this sign is rather "DIM$_4$" than "ŠE." [2)] For lines 1′–2′, cf. KBo 21.1+ I 12–15 (CTH 409.II.1.T.A), KBo 21.2 I 9′ (CTH 409.II.1.T.B), and IBoT 4.22 obv. 3′–5′ (CTH 409.II.1.T.C). Bo 9612 is clearly not the same tablet as KBo 21.2 or IBoT 4.22. [3)] This spelling of ^{NINDA}*mari-* instead of ^{NINDA}*ma-(a)-re-e-eš* / ^{NINDA}*ma-ri-i-iš* is attested only in IBoT 4.22 obv. 1′.

Bo 9614

Description: Mythological.

CTH: 324.3.F "*Telibinu (mugawar)*."

Dating and Script: NS.

Remarks: Bo 9614 is a one-sided fragment from the top portion of a tablet (with upper edge), its lines 1–4 are duplicate to KUB 33.12 IV 7′–11′ (NS), from where the restorations are taken. Further free restorations follow KUB 17.10 IV 24–26.

Measurements: 2.6 × 3.3 × 1.9 cm.

Bibliography: Soysal, *Anatolica* 38, 177 (transliteration).

Bo 9614 (left column)

Left column

§ 1 1 ... (*nu-za* GU$_4$.ḪI.A)] AMAR-*ŠU̥*

2 [*pé-en-ni-iš-ta* (UDU.ḪI.A-*ma-za* SILA$_4$)-*SÚ pé-en-ni-iš*]- *ta* ⌜*x*⌝

3 [(^{d}*Te-li-pí-nu-uš-š*)*a* LUGAL MUNUS.LUGAL DUMU.MEŠ.LUGAL)] *Ù̥* KUR ^{URU}*Ḫa-at-ti*

4 [*pé-en-ni-iš-ta nu-uš-za* (TI-*an-ni i*)]*n-na-ra-u-a*⌊*n*⌋-[(*ni*)]

5 [EGIR.U$_4$-*MI kap-pu-u-e-et*]

(broken off)

Bo 9615 + Bo 8752 + KUB 41.2 + KBo 52.27

Description: Ritual.

CTH: 402.G "*Rituel de Malli, contre la sorcellerie.*"

Dating and Script: MH/NS.

Remarks: Bo 9615 directly joins unpublished fragments Bo 8752 and KUB 41.2 (NS). Bo 9615 + Bo 8752 + I 1–3 are duplicate to KBo 11.12 + KBo 10.43 I 1–4 (MS), KBo 12.126 + KBo 12.127 + KUB 24.9 + I 1–3 (NS) and IBoT 2.123 obv. 1′–3′ (NS), from where the restorations are taken.

Measurements: 1.6 × 3.9 × 2.1 cm.

Bibliography: Soysal, *Anatolica* 38, 182–83 (transliteration and remarks); *Konkordanz,* http://www.hethport.uni-wuerzburg.de/hetskiz/sk.php?f=1058/u.

Bo 9615

Bo 8752 (top left) + Bo 9615 (top right) + KUB 41.2 obv. I (KBo 52.27 is not included)

Obverse I

§ 1 1 [*U*(*M-MA* ^{f}*A-al-li-i* MUNUS)[1)]] ^{URU}*Ar-za-u-u̯a*[2)] *ma-a-an* [(UN-*aš*[3)]) U]Ḫ$_7$-*an-za*[4)] *ną-an kiš-an*[5)]

2 [(*a-ni-i̯a-mi* V ALAM)[6)]] IM ŠÀ-*BA* II LÚ[7)] *nu* ^{KU}[(^{Š}*kur-šu-u*)]*š*[8)] *kạr-pa-an ḫar-kán-zi*

3 [(*na-aš-ta an-da* EME)[9)]].⌊M⌋EŠ[10)] *ki-an-ta-ri*[11)] [ ]

(§§ 2-4 lines 4–11 read as copied in KUB 41.2)

Text-critical notes: [1)] Restoration after KBo 11.12 + I 1. [2)] Duplicate KBo 11.12 + I 1: ^{URU}*Ar-za-u̯i$_5$*. [3)] Restoration follows KBo 12.126 + I 1 and KBo 11.12 + I 1; duplicate KBo 11.12 + I 1: *an-tu-u̯a-ạḫ-ḫạ-aš.* [4)] Duplicate KBo 11.12 + I 2: *al-u̯a-an-za-aḫ-ḫa-an-za.* [5)] Duplicate KBo 11.12 + I 2: *ki-iš-ša-an.* [6)] Restoration after KBo 11.12 + I 2–3. [7)] Duplicate KBo 11.12 + I 3: LÚ.MEŠ. [8)] Restoration follows IBoT 2.123 obv. 2′; duplicates KBo 12.126 + I 2: ^{KUŠ}[*kur*]-*šạ*-[*aš*] and KBo 11.12 + I 3: *kur-šu-uš.* [9)] Restoration after KBo 11.12 + I 4. [10)] Duplicates KBo 11.12 + I 4: EME.ḪI.A and IBoT 2.123 obv. 3′: [E]ME.ḪI.A. [11)] IBoT 2.123 obv. 3′: *ki-i̯a-an-ta-*[*ri*].

Bo 9616

Description: N/A.

CTH: 832 "*Fragments en langue hittite de nature inconnue.*"

Dating and Script: NS.

Remarks: Small, one-sided fragment including the partially inscribed right edge.

Measurements: 3.2 × 1.8 × 2.2 cm.

Bibliography: N/A.

Bo 9616

Bo 9616 (right edge)

§ 1′ 1′]-*x̣ ti-it-*⌊*ta*⌋-[*nu-*

2′] EGIR-*pa*

3′]-*pụ*

4′]-*ẹ-dạ-ni*[1)] *me-ḫu-n*[*i*]

5′]⌊*x x*⌋

(broken off)

Text-critical note: [1)] To be restored either to *kēdani*, *apēdani*, or *kuedani*.

Bo 9617

Description: Ritual or festival.

CTH: 470 "*Fragments de rituels*" or 670 "*Fragments divers.*"

Dating and Script: NS.

Remarks: One-sided fragment.

Measurements: 2.9 × 3.5 × 1.1 cm.

Bibliography: N/A.

Bo 9617

§ 1′ 1′]⌈I? UDU? LUGAL?-ẋ⌉(-)[
2′]-ẋ? LUGAL-*uš* MUNUS.LUGA[L-*aš*?-*ša*
3′] *t*[*i*?-

---

§ 2′ 4′]-*ẋ-ša-ạn* III UDU[1)].ḪI.A *ẋ*-[
5′] *Ạ-NA* DINGIR-*LIM* II TU$_7$ ỤZU(.)[
6′](-)⌊*x-x* ZÌ⌋.DẠ DỤR$_5$(?) 1/2 *ỤP-NI* *ẋ*-[
7′](-)⌊*ḫur*?-*x*⌋-[
(broken off)

Text-critical note: [1)] The sign is not identical with that in line 1′.

Bo 9619

Description: Luwian?.

CTH: 770 "*Fragments en langue louvite.*"

Dating and Script: NS.

Remarks: One-sided fragment in which the script shows almost no clear space between the words.

Measurements: 2.9 × 3.5 × 1.1 cm.

Bibliography: N/A.

Bo 9619

§ 1′	1′	]-⸢*x̣*(-)*x̣*⸣-[
	2′	]-⸢*x k*⸣*at-ti-kụ*?-*x̣*(-)[
	3′	] ⸢*u̯a*?⸣-*ša-an-ta-r*[*i*? 1)
	4′	-*n*]*a*?-*aš-ši-ša-an-t*[*a*?-
	5′	](-)*x̣*(-)*ša-an-t*[*a*-
	6′	](-)*x̣-a-u̯ạ*2)(-)*ša-a-x̣*(-)[
	7′	]⸤*x-x*?-*x̣*⸥[
	(broken off)	

Text-critical notes: 1) Comparing with the sign form "*ti*" in the previous line, this is rather "*ri*" than "*ti*." For the Luwian predicate *waššantari* "they wear," see KUB 9.31 II 23. 2) Perhaps to be read [*n*]*a-a-u̯ạ* for Luwian *nāwa* "not."

Bo 9620

Description: N/A.

CTH: 832 "*Fragments en langue hittite de nature inconnue.*"

Dating and Script: N/A.

Remarks: One-sided fragment that cannot be determined.

Measurements: 3.4 × 2.8 × 1.6 cm.

Bibliography: N/A.

Bo 9620

§ 1′ 1′] *x̣*[

2′]-⸢*x̣*?-*x*⸣ *ar*-*x̣*-[

3′]-⸤*x*⸥-*an*? [1)]-*za* *A-NA* *x̣*(-)[

4′ …

(broken off)

Text-critical note: [1)] The sign is not very clear; it can also be "*pár*."

Bo 9621

Description: N/A.

CTH: 831 "*Fragments en langue inconnue ou indéterminée.*"

Dating and Script: N/A.

Remarks: A one-sided fragment that is moderately abraded and mostly illegible. The preserved signs, as far they can be recognized (e.g., [...](-)*x̣-ḫé-ni a*[*t-*...] in line 4′), and general outlook of the tablet suggest a composition from Boğazköy-Akkadian or Kültepe (Cappadocian) tradition.

Measurements: 3.1 × 2.7 × 1.5 cm.

Bibliography: N/A.

Bo 9621

Bo 9623

Description: N/A.

CTH: 832 "*Fragments en langue hittite de nature inconnue.*"

Dating and Script: OS or MS.

Remarks: One-sided fragment that is too small to classify.

Measurements: 2.4 × 4.0 × 1.1 cm.

Bibliography: N/A.

Bo 9623

§ 1′ 1′](-)⌈*x-x* *x̣*⌉(-)[
2′] *A+NA*[1] [

---

§ 2′ 3′] *nu* *x̣*-[
4′](-)*ne-i̯*[*a*?-
5′](-)⌊*x-ḫi*?-*x-x̣*?⌋(-)[
(broken off)

Text-critical note: [1] Note the old/archaic "ligature" writing of *ANA* here.

Bo 9625

Description: Festival.

CTH: 670 "*Fragments divers.*"

Dating and Script: NS.

Remarks: Small, one-sided fragment.

Measurements: 2.3 × 3.2 × 1.7 cm.

Bibliography: N/A.

Bo 9625

§ 1′ 1′]⌈NINDA.SIG.M⌉EŠ(?)[
2′ I$^{?}$]⌈NINDA.SI⌉G(?) *A-NA* ^{d}UT[U ^{URU}...

---

§ 2′ 3′]-*x̣* I NINDA *dan-na-aš*
4′]-⌊*x̣-za*$^{?}$⌋
5′]-⌊*x̣-ti*$^{?}$⌋
(broken off)

Bo 9626

Description: Prayer$^{?}$.

CTH: 389 "*Fragments de prières.*"

Dating and Script: (L)NS.

Remarks: One-sided fragment.

Measurements: 3.7 × 4.0 × 2.1 cm.

Bibliography: N/A.

Bo 9626

§ 1′ 1′] ⸢*x-x*⸣(-)[
2′]-*x̣-ki-i̯a-aš*(-)[
3′] ⸢*e*$^{?}$*-eš*⸣*-du iš-x̣-*[

---

§ 2′ 4′ ^{U}]^{RU}*Zi-pa-la-an-da*(-)[
5′ KUR ^{U}]^{RU}PA-*ti-ma-za pí-r*[*a*$^{?}$*-an*$^{?}$
6′ *IŠ-T*]*U*(?) *tu-e-da-za a-aš-š*[*i*$^{?}$-[1)]

---

§ 3′ 7′ ^{UR}]^{U}*Zi-p*⌞*a*⌟*-l*⌞*a-a*⌟*n-da x̣*[2)]-[
8′]-⌞*x-za*$^{?}$⌟*-a-i*(-)*x̣*$^{?}$(-)[
9′]-⌞*x*⌟ [
(broken off)

Text-critical notes: [1)] Possibly to be restored as *a-aš-š*[*i-i̯a-an-da-za* …] "from your bel[oved … (place)]"; cf. KUB 36.90 obv. 20′ and rev. 32′–33′ (*tu-e-da-az a-aš-ši-i̯a-an-ta-za* / *a-aš-ši-i̯a-an-da-az*). [2)] Perhaps to be reconstructed as [… ^{d}U / ^{d}IŠKUR ^{UR}]^{U}*Zi-p*⌞*a*⌟*-l*⌞*a-a*⌟*n-da* E[N-*YA*] "[O Stormgod of] Zipalanda, [my] lo[rd]."

Bo 9627

Description: N/A.

CTH: 832 "*Fragments en langue hittite de nature inconnue.*"

Dating and Script: NH/NS.

Remarks: One-sided fragment that contains a royal genealogy including the name of Muršili II. The precise text genre cannot be determined.

Measurements: 3.5 × 5.5 × 1.4 cm.

Bibliography: N/A.

Bo 9627

§ 1′ 1′ ^{m}*Mu-u*]⌈*r-ši-l*⌉*i* LUGAL.[GAL …$^{?}$]
2′ […$^{?}$ LUGAL KUR ^{URU}*Ḫ*]*a-at-ti* UR.SAG [

---

§ 2′ 3′ a (illegible, erased$^{?}$ signs)
3′ b]⌊*x-x-x-x*⌋[
(broken off)

Bo 9628 + KUB 36.75 + Bo 9659

Description: Prayer.

CTH: 374.2.A "*Analogues aux précédentes* (i.e., CTH 372–373)."

Dating and Script: MH/MS.

Remarks: Bo 9628 lines 1′–4′ directly join KUB 36.75 II 21′–24′ (MS), and Bo 9659 II 4′–6′, an anonymous royal prayer to the Sungod. Bo 9628 + KUB 36.75 II 21′–25′ are parallel to the Kantuzzili Prayer KUB 30.10 rev. 14–16 (CTH 373.A) as well as KUB 30.11+ rev. 10′–12′ (CTH 374.1). See also under Bo 9659 + KUB 36.75 + and cover.

Measurements: 2.5 × 3.9 × 1.3 cm.

Bibliography: N/A.

Bo 9628

KUB 36.75 + Bo 9659 + Bo 9628 obv. II

Obverse II

(Line numbers of Bo 9628 are in parentheses)

…

§ 9′ 21′ (= 1′) *nu* É-*YA* ⸢*i*⸣*š-ḫa-aḫ-ru-*[*u̯*]*a-aš*[1)] É-*YA*
22′ (= 2′) ⸢*ki-i-ša*⸣- *a̤t*

---

§ 10′ 23′ (= 3′) [*nu*(-)…] *pí̤t-tu̯-li-iš-ki-mi* ZI-*YA-p*[*át-ma*]
24′ (= 4′) [*ta-ma-a*]*t-ta pé-e-di za-ap-pí-iš-ki-i̯*[*z-zi*]

---

§ 11′ 25′ (= 5′) [*nu* MU-*t*]⸢*i*?⸣ *me-e*⸣*-ni-aš ar-ma-a-*[*la-aš ma-a-aḫ-ḫa-an*[2)]
(broken off)

Text-critical notes: [1)] Contra *pít-tu-li-i̯a-aš* in KUB 30.10 rev. 14, this reading follows a recent direct join with Bo 9659, and the whole sentence reads "my house became my house of tea[r]s." [2)] KUB 36.75 + III 14′, 19′, 21′, IV 13′ always uses this form with *a*-plene writing; cf. Lebrun, *Hymnes*, 131.

Bo 9630

Description: Ritual.

CTH: 394.I "*Rituel d'Ashella, contre une épidémie dans l'armée.*"

Dating and Script: MH/NS or LNS.

Remarks: Bo 9630 is a one-sided fragment whose lines 2′–4′ are duplicate to KUB 9.31 III 63 (CTH 394.C), KUB 41.17 III 12′–14′ (CTH 410.C), KBo 13.212:9′–10′ (CTH 394.B) (all NS), from where the restorations are taken.

Measurements: 2.6 × 3.7 × 2.0 cm.

Bibliography: N/A.

Bo 9630

§ 1′ 1′]-*x̣* *x̣*-[

2′] $^{\text{⸢UZU⸣}}$Ì NINDA.GU⸢R$_4$⸣.[(RA.ḪI.A)

3′ (*IŠ-TU* KAŠ GA)]L.ḪI.A ^{DUG}GÌ[(R.GÁN)

4′ (*ki-iš-ša-an me-ma-aḫ-ḫ*)]*i* *ka*-⸤*a-š*⸥[*a*(-)[1)]

5′]-⸤*x*⸥ [

(broken off)

Text-critical note: [1)] This reading is due to the visible signs shown here. Thus, revise the reconstruction [(*me-ma-aḫ*)-*ḫa-an-zi ka-aš-ma-u̯a*] posed by Dinçol, *Belleten* XLIX/193, 17.

Bo 9631

Description: N/A.
CTH: 832 "*Fragments en langue hittite de nature inconnue.*"
Dating and Script: NS.
Remarks: One-sided fragment that is not to be identified.
Measurements: 2.3 × 3.2 × 1.8 cm.
Bibliography: N/A.

Bo 9631

§ 1′ 1′] ⌈*ki-iš-ša-a*⌉[*n*
2′ *ka*?]-*a-ša-u̯a pí-x̣-*[
3′ *ar-ḫ*]*a šar-ni-i*[*n-kán*? 1)-
4′ *k*]*a-ạ-š*⸤*a*(?)⸥(-)[
5′] ⸤*x̣*⸥ [
(broken off)

Text-critical note: 1) Or as an iterative form *šar-ni-i*[*n-ki-*...] ?

Bo 9632

Description: Hattian-Hittite bilingual benediction.

CTH: 736.9 "*Paroles de la Zintuhi dans le temple du Soleil* (*en partie bilingue*)."

Dating and Script: NS or LNS.

Remarks: Bo 9632, a piece of the right-bottom and upper parts of the tablet, belongs to the well-known Hattian-Hittite bilingual text. It contains the Hittite portions only: obv. II$^{?}$ 5′–6′ are duplicate or parallel to KBo 37.48(+)KUB 28.8 obv. rt. col. 1′–3′ (NS), KBo 17.22 III 4′ (OS) and KBo 56.186:1′–2′ (NS) from where the restorations are taken; rev. III$^{?}$ 1–5 are analogous to KBo 37.48(+)KUB 28.8 obv. rt. col. 4′–8′ and KBo 17.22 III 5′–9′.

Measurements: 2.6 × 3.2 × 2.2 cm.

Bibliography: Soysal, *Anatolica* 38, 188–89 (transliteration and remarks).

Bo 9632 obv. II$^{?}$

Bo 9632 rev. III$^{?}$

Bo 9632 rev. III? (right edge)

Obverse II?

§ 1′ 1′ (traces)

---

§ 2′ 2′]-⌈*un*?⌉[1)]

3′]-⌈*ur*?⌉-*tẹ-pu-uš*[2)]

4′]-*x̣* KẠR-*at*?[3)]

5′ -*i̯*]*a* LUGAL-*un* MUNUS.LUGAL-*na*

6′ KUR-*e-i̯a-a*(*n-ti ḫu-u-ma-an*)-*t*]*i* LUGAL.MEŠ[4)] DÙ-*ạt*[5)]

(bottom of the tablet)

Reverse III?

§ 1 1]-*x̣* KUR-[…?]-*x*?-*x̣ ịš-x̣*-[…]

2 *d*]*a*?-*a-šu̯-ẹš x̣-x̣-x̣*(-)[…?]

3 *d*]*a-a-aš nu la-ba-ar*-⸤*na*⸥-[*a*]*š*?

4]-*x̣ da-ạ-lu-ga-aš*

5] ⸤*ạ-ša*⸥-*an-du*

6 (traces)

(broken off)

Text-critical notes: [1)] To be restored [LUGAL]-⌈*un*⌉ like in II? 5′; cf. the possible Hattian counterpart *ka-a-at-ti* in KBo 37.49 rev. 11′. [2)] Cf. the possible Hattian counterpart *u̯u$_u$-u-ur-te-pu-uš* (= *wu$_u$r⸗te⸗pu⸗š*) in KBo 37.49 rev. 12′. [3)] This is the (L)NH spelling of *wemiyat* "found; arrived"; this could be the Hittite translation of the Hattian verbal form *tu-ut-ḫe-el* (= *tu⸗t⸗ḫel*) in KBo 37.49 rev. 12′. [4)] Cf. the possible Hattian counterpart [*u̯u$_u$-u*(?)]-*ru-un te-u̯a$_a$-ka-at-ti* (= *wu$_u$r⸗un te⸗wa$_a$⸗katti*) in KBo 37.49 rev. 13′. [5)] This is the (L)NH spelling of *iyat* "made"; this seems to be the Hittite translation of the Hattian verbal form *tu̯-u-u̯a$_a$-ạp-*[*pu*] (= *tu⸗wa$_a$⸗pu*) in KBo 37.49 rev. 12′. Other versions KBo 37.48(+)KUB 28.8 obv. rt. col. 3′ and KBo 17.22 III 4′ have the older spelling *i-e-et* instead.

Bo 9634

Description: Kizzuwatnan ritual.

CTH: 500 “*Fragments de rituels (ou de fêtes) du Kizzuwatna.*”

Dating and Script: NS or LNS.

Remarks: Small, one-sided fragment from the left column of a tablet that contains only Hurrian words.

Measurements: 1.9 × 4.2 × 2.0 cm.

Bibliography: N/A.

Bo 9634

§ 1′ 1′](-)⸢*x̣-x-x-u̯i*⸣*ᵢ* [...?]

2′]⸤G⸥U₄*še-e-ri-šu-u*⸢*š*⸣ [1)]

3′]-⸤*x̣-u̯*⸥*aₐ*

4′]-*x̣*

5′]-⸤*x*⸥

(broken off)

Text-critical note: 1) For this spelling, cf. *še-ri-šu-uš* in Hurrian context KBo 23.33+ IV 7′, however without having the determinative GU₄. Thus, also containing only Hurrian words, Bo 9634 is reminiscent of the composition of KBo 23.33+ (CTH 778.I.1.A).

Bo 9635

Description: N/A.

CTH: 832 "*Fragments en langue hittite de nature inconnue.*"

Dating and Script: NS or LNS.

Remarks: Small fragment from the upper- and lower-right portions (with edges) of a tablet that is too small to classify.

Measurements: 3.4 × 2.2 × 2.0 cm.

Bibliography: N/A.

Bo 9635 obv.?

Bo 9635 rev.$^{?}$

Bo 9635 rev.$^{?}$

Bo 9635 rev.$^{?}$ (right edge)

Obverse$^{?}$

§ 1	1	] *gur*[1)]*-dạ-lị*(?)*-x̣*$^{?}$
	2	…
	______________________	
§ 2	3–4	(illegible signs)
	(broken off)	

Reverse$^{?}$

§ 1′	1′	]*-x̣-na-an-zi*
	2′	]*-x̣-an-na-i*
	3′	…
	(bottom of the tablet)	

Text-critical note: [1)] This reading of the sign is uncertain, but more likely than "*e*." Because of the suggested lemma $^{(GI/GIŠ)}$*gurdali-* (a wooden container) one may expect here a text of religious nature.

Bo 9636

Description: N/A.

CTH: 832 "*Fragments en langue hittite de nature inconnue.*"

Dating and Script: LNS.

Remarks: One-sided small fragment from the upper portion of a tablet including the upper edge.

Measurements: 1.5 × 4.7 × 2.3 cm.

Bibliography: N/A.

Bo 9636

§ 1′ 1′]-*x̣* MU.KAM.ḪI.A GÍD.DA *nu*(-)*x̣*(-)[1)][

2′](-)⌊*x*⌋-*x̣*-*i̯a*-*a*⌊*n* MU⌋.KAM.ḪI.Ạ GÍ[D.DA(?)

(broken off)

Text-critical note: [1)] Or to be read logographic NU.x̣ ? Cf. MU.ḪI.A GÍD.DA *nu-ú-un* (KBo 2.9 + I 21′), but also *nu-kán ANA* MỤ.ḪI.A GÍD.DA NU.SIG_5 (oracular text KBo 41.211 lt. col. 5′).

Bo 9637 + Bo 9569 + KUB 15.33b +

Description: Evocation ritual.

CTH: 483.II.A "*Rituel: 'quand on tire les dieux sur les chemins.'*"

Dating and Script: MH/LNS.

Remarks: Bo 9637 is a one-sided fragment whose lines 1′–9′ directly join Bo 9569:3′–5′ and KUB 15.33b IV 1′–7′ (LNS). Bo 9637 + Bo 9569 + KUB 15.33b IV 26–34 are parallel to KUB 15.34 IV 39′–47′ (MS), from where the restorations are taken. See also under: Bo 9569 + Bo 9637 + KUB 15.33b +; Bo 9571 + KUB 15.38 + Bo 10125 +.

Measurements: 3.6 × 3.6 × 1.1 cm.

Bibliography: *Konkordanz,* http://www.hethport.uni-wuerzburg.de/hetskiz/sk.php?f=Bo%2069/264.

Bo 9637

Bo 9569 + Bo 9637 + rev. IV

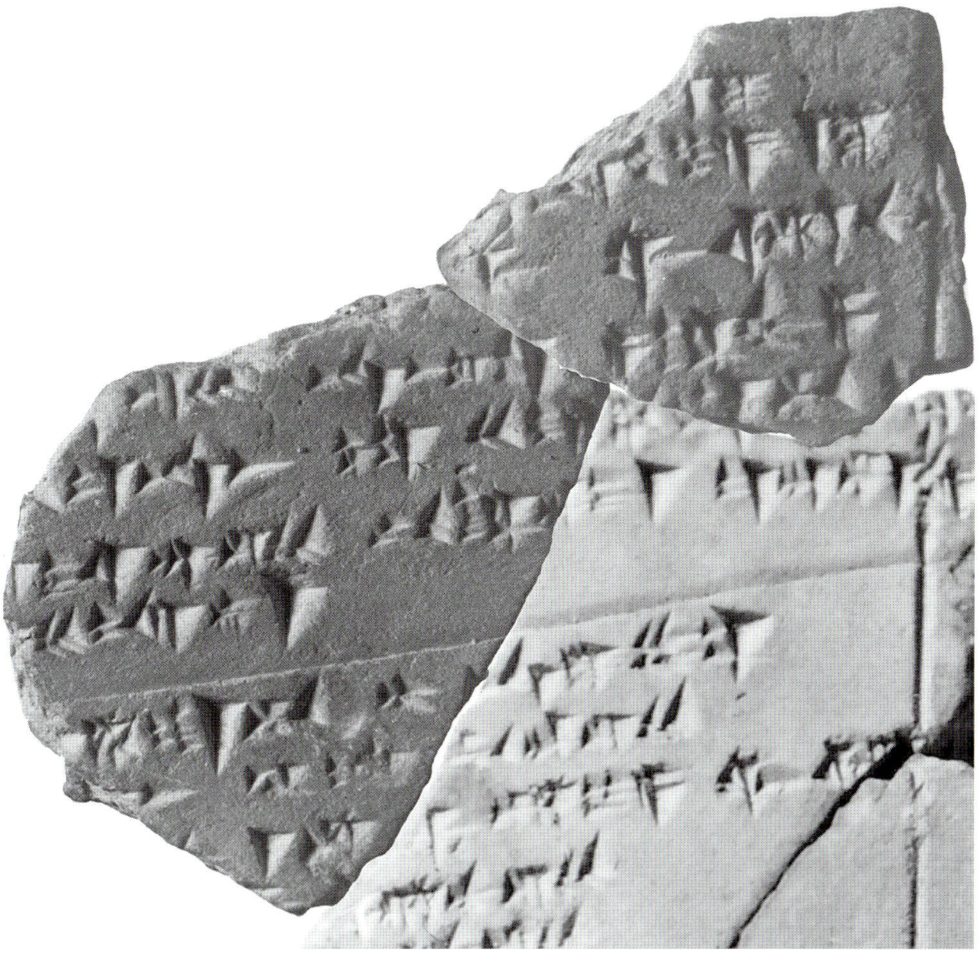

Bo 9569 + Bo 9637 + KUB 15.33b + rev. IV (composite image)

Bo 9571 + Bo 10125 + Bo 9637 + Bo 9569 rev. IV

Reverse IV

(Line numbering follows KUB 15.38+; line numbers of Bo 9637 are in parentheses)

§ 3 26 (= 1′) [*z*]⸤*u-uz*⸥-[*zu-ma*]-⸤*ki-i̯a ke-e*⸥[*l-di-i̯a am-b*]⸢*a*$^?$*-aš*$^?$⸣-[*š*]*i u̯a-ar-nu-z*[*i*[1)]]

27 (= 2′) [*zé-e-a-an-ti-t*]*a QA-TAM-MA* ⸢*ir*⸣-[*ḫa-a-i*]⸢*z-zi*⸣ [2)] *na-aš-tạ a-ra-aḫ-za*

28 (= 3′) [*aš-nu-ut-ta-at n*]*u* DINGIR.MEŠ MUNUS.MEŠ LUGA⸢L-*u*⸣-*iz-na-aš ŠA* KUR ^{URU}*Ḫa-at-ti*[3)] *šạ-r*[*a-a*]

29 (= 4′) [*ta-an-zi na-aš-k*]*án ša-ra-a ụ́-da-an-zi pí-ra-an-ma* GIŠ ^{d}INANNA.ḪI.A

30 (= 5′) [*ar-ga-a-mi gal-gal-t*]*u-u-ri ḫa-a*[*z-z*]*i-iš-kán-* [*zi*]

---

§ 4 31 (= 6′) [*nu* DINGIR.MEŠ MUNUS.MEŠ LUGAL-*u-iz*]-⸤*na*⸥-*aš* [*ŠA* KUR ^{UR}]^{U}*Ḫa-at-ti*[4)] *tar-na-lu-li*[5)]

32 (= 7′) [*pé-e-ta-an-zi* DINGIR.MEŠ LÚ.MEŠ ^{GIŠ}ERI]N-*aš kat-tạ ti-an-zi*

33 (= 8′) [*nu-uš-ma-aš kat-ta-an iš-ḫu-u̯a-an-zi n*]*u* I MUŠEN *u̯u*$_{u}$*-ri-i̯a u̯a-a*⸤*r*⸥-[*nu-zi*[6)]]

34 (= 9′) [I MUŠEN *a-ša-ap-ši-i̯a ḫi-iš-ša-am-mi-ši-i̯a u̯*]*a-ar-nu-zi*[7)]

…

(Bo 9537 breaks off here; the text after [*u̯*]*a-ar-nu-zi* continues in the following lines of KUB 15.33b)

Text-critical notes: [1)] KUB 15.34 IV 40′: *u̯a-ar-nu-an-zi*. [2)] KUB 15.34 IV 40′: *ir-ḫa-a-zi*. [3)] KUB 15.34 IV 41′ has DINGIR.MEŠ LÚ.MEŠ ^{GIŠ}ERIN-*aš* instead. [4)] KUB 15.34 IV 44′ has DINGIR.MEŠ LÚ.MEŠ ^{GIŠ}ERIN-*aš* instead. [5)] KUB 15.34 IV 44′ adds -*i̯a*. [6)] KUB 15.34 IV 46′: *u̯a-ar-nu-an-zi*. [7)] KUB 15.34 IV 47′: *u̯a-ar-nu-an-zi*.

Bo 9638

Description: Ritual or festival.

CTH: 470 "*Fragments de rituels*" or 670 "*Fragments divers.*"

Dating and Script: NS.

Remarks: Small, one-sided fragment.

Measurements: 2.7 × 2.8 × 1.3 cm.

Bibliography: N/A.

Bo 9638

§ 1′ 1′](-)⸢*x-x*(-)*ar*⸣(-)[
2′ (-)*te*$^{?}$]-*e-pu* [
3′] *ḫạ-ạt-ti-li*(-)[
4′ *me-ma*(?)]- *i*[1)] [
(broken off)

Text-critical note: [1)] Or: [*ḫal-za-a*(?)]-*i*.

Bo 9639

Description: Festival.
CTH: 670 "*Fragments divers.*"
Dating and Script: NS.
Remarks: One-sided fragment.
Measurements: 4.5 × 2.1 × 0.9 cm.
Bibliography: N/A.

Bo 9639

§ 1′	1′	]-*x̣ x*$^{?}$-[
	2′	-*a*]*n*$^{?}$-*z*[*i*
	3′	]-*x̣* EZẸ[N(-)
	4′	]-*x̣-ša-a*[*t*(-)
	5′	-*e*]*š-ša* DINGI⸢R.MEŠ⸣[(-)
	6′	]-*x̣-aš A-NA x̣*(./-)[
	7′	^{LÚ}]*a̯-ra-aš* ^{LÚ}*a̯*-[*ra*$^{?}$-*an*$^{?}$ [1)]
	8′	^{LÚ}]*a̯-ra-aš-ša x̣*-[
	9′	](-)*x̣-u̯a-ar-x̣*-[
	10′	$^{LÚ?}$]SANGA *x̣*-[
	11′	] DINGIR-*L*⸤*UM*⸥(-)[
	(broken off)	

Text-critical note: [1)] Cf. KUB 20.88 I$^{?}$ 1; or to be completed with the dative form ^{LÚ}*a̯*-[*ri*] (KUB 45.49 IV 7).

Bo 9640

Description: Ritual.

CTH: 470 "*Fragments de rituels*."

Dating and Script: NS.

Remarks: One-sided fragment.

Measurements: 3.4 × 2.9 × 1.5 cm.

Bibliography: N/A.

Bo 9640

§ 1′ 1′]⌈*x-x-x-x*⌉[
2′ *-m*]*a?-an* ⌈ ⌉(eras.) *x̣*-[
3′]-*x̣ ḫu-u-lạ*-[*li-i̯a?-zi?*

---

§ 2′ 4′ *-i̯*]*a?-an* SAG.DU-*Š*⌈*U*⌉[
5′]-*x̣-an pu-u-tal-l*[*i-*[1)]
6′] *Ị?-EN QA-TỊ?*(-)*x̣?*(-)[
7′]-*kụ-un*(-)*x̣*(-)[
8′ (-)*k*]*a?*-⌊*ta*⌋-[
(broken off)

Text-critical note: [1)] This incomplete word with plene-spelling *pu-u-* belongs to *putalliya-* "to tie (together)"; CHD P/3 (1997) 401 ff.

Bo 9641

Description: N/A.

CTH: 832 "*Fragments en langue hittite de nature inconnue.*"

Dating and Script: NS.

Remarks: One-sided fragment that is too small to classify.

Measurements: 4.0 × 4.5 × 1.7 cm.

Bibliography: N/A.

Bo 9641

§ 1′ 1′ -*i*]*š*?(-)*nu*(-)[
2′ …

---

§ 2′ 3′ -*k*]*i*?-*it*(-)[
4′](-)*x̣*-*x̣*-*du*-*x̣*(-)[
5′](-)*x̣*-*x̣*-*zị* *n*[*a*-
6′] ŠEŠ?-*YA*(-)[
7′]⸢*x*⸣[
(broken off)

Bo 9642

Description: N/A.

CTH: 832 "*Fragments en langue hittite de nature inconnue*."

Dating and Script: NS.

Remarks: One-sided fragment that is too small to determine.

Measurements: 5.4 × 1.6 × 1.8 cm.

Bibliography: N/A.

Bo 9642

§ 1′	1′	(traces)
	2′	]-*x̣-dạ* *x̣*-[
	3′	] *te-ez-z*[*i*
	4′	-*k*]*i*$^{?}$-*iš-k*⸢*i*⸣-[
	5′	]-*ši k*[*a*$^{?}$-
	6′	-*m*]*a*$^{?}$ *x̣*-[
	7′	-*r*]*i*$^{?}$-*i̯*[*a*(-)
	8′	(traces)
	(broken off)	

Bo 9643

Description: N/A.

CTH: 832 "*Fragments en langue hittite de nature inconnue.*"

Dating and Script: N/A.

Remarks: One-sided fragment of the upper-edge portion of a tablet; too small to determine.

Measurements: 2.6 × 4.9 × 2.6 cm.

Bibliography: N/A.

Bo 9643

§ 1 1 (traces)
2](-)*ẋ*?-*ẋ* *ẋ*(-)*ẋ*-*ẋ*-*ẋ*(-)*ẋ*-*ẋ*-*ẋ*-*nị*? *an-dạ*
3](-)⌊*ẋ*?(-)*a*⌋*r-ra-i*
4](-)⌊*x-ḫ*⌋*a*?
(broken off)

Bo 9644

Description: Festival$^{?}$.

CTH: 670 "*Fragments divers.*"$^{?}$

Dating and Script: (L)NS.

Remarks: One-sided fragment.

Measurements: 3.9 × 3.6 × 1.4 cm.

Bibliography: N/A.

Bo 9644

§ 1′ 1′]⸢*x* *x̣*⸣[

2′ -*i̯*]*a-at-t*⸢*a*⸣(-)[

3′]-*x̣-uš* *pí-i-ẹ*-[

4′]-*x̣-ni*$^{?}$ *i-i̯a-a*⸢*n-t*⸣[*a*(-)

5′ I]⌊GI$^{?}$⌋.ḪI.A-*u̯a* [...$^{?}$]

---

§ 2′ 6′ *UŠ-K*]⌊*E*⌋(?)-*EN*

7′ (-)*a*]⌊*n*$^{?}$⌋-*da*(-)[

(broken off)

Bo 9645

Description: Ritual[?].

CTH: 470 "*Fragments de rituels*[?]."

Dating and Script: NS.

Remarks: One-sided fragment, including a part of the right edge.

Measurements: 6.2 × 2.0 × 2.5 cm.

Bibliography: N/A.

Bo 9645

§ 1′ 1′]-*x̣*[?]
2′ …
3′]-*x̣* *ḫu-da-ak* *x̣*[1)]
4′ -*z*]*i*
5′ …

---

§ 2′ 4′]-*i*
5′ …
6′](-)*an-da da-a-i*
7′]-*x̣* GAR-*ri*
8′] ZALAG.GA.A(?)
9′–10′ …

---

§ 3′ 11′]-⌊*x̣*⌋ *ki-i*
12′ -*š*]*ar-i̯a*[2)]
(broken off)

Text-critical notes: [1)] This sign is from other side of the tablet. [2)] More probably a plant name, […^{S}]^{AR}-*i̯a*.

Bo 9646

Description: Ritual or festival.

CTH: 470 "*Fragments de rituels*" or 670 "*Fragments divers.*"

Dating and Script: NS.

Remarks: One-sided fragment.

Measurements: 4.6 × 2.4 × 0.8 cm.

Bibliography: N/A.

Bo 9646

§ 1′ 1′]-*x̣-ti-i̯a* [
2′]-*x̣-ma* ^{MUNUS}ŠU.G[I(-)
3′ *pí-r*]*a-an kat-t*[*a*
4′]-*x̣* GAL.GEŠTIN [
5′ -*n*]*i*$^{?}$ *ši-pa-a*[*n*-

---

§ 2′ 6′ -*n*]*a*$^{?}$ [
7′ -*a*]*n* [
8′ -*p*]*a-a*[*n*(-)
9′]-*a*[*n*(-)
(broken off)

Bo 9647 + KUB 35.13

Description: Ritual.

CTH: 763 "*Fragments de rituels hittites contenant des louvismes.*"

Dating and Script: NS.

Remarks: Bo 9647 is a one-sided fragment whose lines 2′–6′ directly join KUB 35.13:6′–10′ (NS).

Measurements: 2.7 × 2.5 × 1.3 cm.

Bibliography: Soysal, *Anatolica* 38, 190 (transliteration).

Bo 9647

Bo 9647 + KUB 35.13 (composite image)

(Line numbers of Bo 9647 are in parentheses)

§ 1′ 5′ (= 1′) (traces)

6′ (= 2′) [...$^{?}$ EGI]⸢R$^{?}$⸣-*ạn-dạ* [X]⸤X$^{?}$ ^{GI}⸥^{Š}GAG.ḪI.A ZABAR XX $^{\text{GI!Š}}$[GAG.ḪI.A

7′ (= 3′) [...$^{?}$] X̣XX$^{?}$ [1)] ^{GIŠ}GAG.ḪI.A [G]IŠ-*ru-u̯a-aš da-a-i* [

8′ (= 4′) [...$^{?}$] *nu-uš-ma-aš i-da-la-a-mu-uš na-ak-k*[*i-uš* ...$^{?}$]

9′ (= 5′) [...$^{?}$] *kat-ta tar-ma-a-*⸢*iz*⸥*-zi* ^{MUNUS}ŠU.GI *lu-*⸤*ú*⸥*-*[*i-li*]

10′ (= 6′) [2)]] *k*⸢*i-i*⸣*š-ša-an* ⸢ ⸥ <*me*>[3)]*-ma-i*

---

§ 2′ 11′ (= 7′)]⸤ *x-x-x-x*$^{?}$⸥[ ]-*x̣ a-ša-an-d*[*u*

(broken off)

Text-critical notes: [1)] The number consists of three *winkelhakens*, thus "XXX," differently from "XX" in KUB 35.13:6′. [2)] It seems no other word is written in this lacuna. [3)] Immediately following an erasure, the sign "*me*" has apparently been erased, or dropped out by accident.

Bo 9648

Description: N/A.

CTH: 832 "*Fragments en langue hittite de nature inconnue.*"

Dating and Script: NS$^{?}$.

Remarks: Small, one-sided fragment from the right portion (with edge) of a tablet that cannot be identified.

Measurements: 3.5 × 3.8 × 1.6 cm.

Bibliography: N/A.

Bo 9648

§ 1′ 1′]-⌈*x*⌉

2′]-*x̣*

---

§ 2′ 3′]-*x̣ nu a-pu-u-u̯n*

4′]-*x̣*$^{?}$-*u̯a-an kat-ta*

5′]-*x̣-kán-* ⌊*x̣*⌋

6′]-⌊*xx̣*$^{?}$ *ma-a*⌋[*ḫ*(?)-

(broken off)

Bo 9650

Description: Mythological.

CTH: 341.III.22 "*Gilgameš. Version hittite*"

Dating and Script: NH/NS.

Remarks: One-sided fragment. The narrative in Bo 9650 gives a conversation of Šanḫatu with [Enkidu$^{?}$], and this is in close affiliation with KUB 8.55(+) II 1′–7′ // KUB 8.51(+) rev. 5′–9′ (CTH 341.III.1.B+D and III.1.C), translated by G. Beckman, "The Hittite Gilgamesh," in *The Epic of Gilgamesh*, edited by B. R. Foster (New York: Norton, 2001), 159. The exact placement of Bo 9650 within the text complex, however, is not possible.

Measurements: 3.2 × 3.8 × 2.0 cm.

Bibliography: N/A.

Bo 9650

§ 1′ 1′ (traces)

2′ *ku-e*(?)]-*ẹl-gạ* URU-*rị*$^{?}$(-)*x̣*$^{?}$-*x̣*(-)[

3′]-*šị ḫạ-lu-gạ-aš*[1)] *ịš-x̣*-[

4′ *A-NA* ^{f}]*Ša-an-ḫa-du*[2)] EGỊ[R-*pa me-mi-iš-ki-iz-zi*

5′](.)⸤B⸥ÚN-*aš*[3)] *nu* ^{f}*Ša-a*[*n-ḫa-du-uš*

6′ EGIR-*pa me*]-*mị-iš-ki-ịz*-[*zi*

7′ (traces)

(broken off)

Text-critical notes: [1)] Likewise read in KUB 8.55(+) II 2′: ⸢*ḫa*$^{?}$-*lu*$^{?}$-*ga*⸣-*aš* ? [2)] The name of ^{f}*Ša-an-ḫa-du* (conventional transliteration "*tù*"), the harlot, can be restored with a combination of the following line and it is attested only in this fragment in its complete form among other Hittite fragments of the Gilgameš epic. [3)] Despite the visible clear signs BÚN(= KA×IM)-*aš*, this incomplete word is not to be understood within the present context and could be a part of a longer logogram; syntactically compare with ⸢*ḫa*$^{?}$-*lu*$^{?}$-*ga*⸣-*aš nu* ^{f}*Ša-an-ḫ*[*a-du-*...] in KUB 8.55(+) II 2′ (readings based on two tablet photos: *hethiter.net/:PhotArch N04629* and *hethiter.net/:PhotArch BoFN00674d*).

Bo 9651

Description: Ritual or festival.

CTH: 470 "*Fragments de rituels*" or 670 "*Fragments divers*."

Dating and Script: NS.

Remarks: One-sided fragment.

Measurements: 2.2 × 2.6 × 1.1 cm.

Bibliography: N/A.

Bo 9651

§ 1′ …

——

§ 2′ 1′](-)*x̣* LÚSANGA-*a*⌈*n*⌉[1)][

2′ *a-p*]*a*(?)-*a-aš-ša* III-*Š*[*U*

3′]-*zi na-aš-ta x̣*-[

4″ …

————————————————

§ 3′ 5″ -*k*]*án k*[*u*-

6″]⌊*x*⌋[

(broken off)

Text-critical note: [1)] Or: LÚSANGA ⌈d⌉[…].

Bo 9652

Description: Historical?.

CTH: 215 "*Fragments non caractérisés.*"

Dating and Script: (E)NS.

Remarks: One-sided fragment.

Measurements: 3.1 × 4.4 × 1.5 cm.

Bibliography: N/A.

Bo 9652

§ 1′ 1′ *-a]t-r[a-*[1]
2′ *I-N]⌜A⌝* $^{\text{ḪUR.SAG}}$*A[r-*

---

§ 2′ 3′ *-i]n*? [2] *I-NA* $^{\text{ḪUR.SA}}$⸤^{G}*A*⸥*[r*?-
4′ *]-ak-ta*[3] ⸤*x̣*⸥-[
5′ ^{URU}*Ka*? [4]*]-az-za-p[a(-)*
6′ *]-x̣ Ú-[UL*?
(broken off)

Text-critical notes: [1] Belongs to the verb *ḫatrai-* "to write"? [2] Maybe to be restored as *[tu-uz-zi-i]n.* [3] *[a]-ak-ta* or *[ḫar]-ak-ta* ? [4] Or spelled as ^{URU}*Ga-*°.

Bo 9653

Description: N/A.

CTH: 832 "*Fragments en langue hittite de nature inconnue.*"

Dating and Script: Murš. II/NS.

Remarks: One-sided fragment that is too small to classify. The text could be of historical, but also of religious nature (cf. CTH 482 and 486), bearing the name of Muršili II.

Measurements: 1.5 × 4.4 × 2.0 cm.

Bibliography: N/A.

Bo 9653 obv.

Obverse

§ 1 1]⸢d⸣UTU-*ŠI* m*Mur-ši*-DINGIR-*LIM* LUG[AL.GAL

2]-⸢*x*⸣ *ma-a-a*⸢*n* *x*⸣-[

3]⸢*x̣* *x̣*⸣[

(broken off)

Bo 9654

Description: Ritual or festival$^{?}$.

CTH: 470 "*Fragments de rituels*" or 670 "*Fragments divers.*"

Dating and Script: (L)NS.

Remarks: Tiny fragment including a portion of the inscribed upper edge.

Measurements: 1.7 × 4.8 × 2.6 cm.

Bibliography: N/A.

Bo 9654

§ 1′ 1′]-*x̣*$^{?}$ *A-NA* IX ^{GIŠ}MAR.GÍD.DA.ḪI.[A

2′] *da-a-i*⸤*š-ta-an*⸥(-) [...$^{?}$]

(broken off)

Bo 9657

Description: Ritual or festival.

CTH: 470 "*Fragments de rituels*" or 670 "*Fragments divers.*"

Dating and Script: NS.

Remarks: Small, one-sided fragment.

Measurements: 4.0 × 2.3 × 0.9 cm.

Bibliography: N/A.

Bo 9657

§ 1′ 1′]-⸢*x̣-an*?⸣ [

2′ -*š*]*a*?-*an* [

3′]-*x̣ da-a-ị*

---

§ 2′ 4′]-*x̣*

5′]-*x̣* TUR-*TIM*

6′ -*u̯*]*a*?-*az*

7′]-*x̣*- *zi*

8′ -*š*]*i*?-*i̯a*

9′]⸤ *x* *x* ⸥

(broken off)

Bo 9658

Description: N/A.

CTH: 832 "*Fragments en langue hittite de nature inconnue.*"

Dating and Script: NS.

Remarks: One-sided fragment from the right column of a tablet.

Measurements: 1.8 × 2.3 × 1.0 cm.

Bibliography: N/A.

Bo 9658

Right column

§ 1′ 1′ ${}^{\text{É}}$*tar-nu-u-ẹ-e*[*š*${}^{?}$(-)[1]

2′ ${}^{\text{GIŠ}}$KIRI$_6$.ḪI.A-*aš* [

3′ *ŠA* ${}^{\text{GIŠ}}$KIRI$_6$(.)[

4′ *ḫu-u-ma-ạn-d*[*u-uš*(-)

5′ ⸤*x-x-x*⸥(-)[

(broken off)

Text-critical note: [1] For this spelling of the word, see KUB 13.2+ II 13′. The co-attestation of ${}^{\text{É}}$*tarnu-* "cultic bath house or booth" with ${}^{\text{GIŠ}}$KIRI$_6$.GEŠTIN "vineyard" and / or ${}^{\text{GIŠ}}$KIRI$_6$.SAR "kitchen-garden" occurs in KUB 13.2+ II 19′ (CTH 261.1.A; instruction) and KBo 38.206 obv. 14′–15′ (CTH 470.911; ritual).

Bo 9659 + KUB 36.75 + Bo 9628

Description: Prayer.

CTH: 374.2.A "*Analogues aux précédentes* (i.e., CTH 372–373)."

Dating and Script: MH/MS.

Remarks: Bo 9659 lines 1′–6′ directly join KUB 36.75 II 18′–21′ (MS), and unpublished fragment Bo 9628 II 1′–3′, an anonymous royal prayer to the Sungod. Bo 9659 + KUB 36.75 II 18′–23′ are parallel to the Kantuzzili Prayer KUB 30.10 rev. 12–15 (CTH 373.A) as well as KUB 30.11+ rev. 9′–11′ (CTH 374.1). See also under Bo 9628 + KUB 36.75 +.

Measurements: 3.3 × 4.5 × 1.4 cm.

Bibliography: Soysal, *Anatolica* 38, 179–80 (transliteration and remarks); *Konkordanz*, http://www.hethport.uni-wuerzburg.de/hetskiz/sk.php?f=1226/u.

KUB 36.75 + Bo 9659 obv. II (detail)

KUB 36.75 + Bo 9659 obv. II (lower part)

Bo 4696 + KUB 36.75 + KBo 52.13 + Bo 9659 obv. I and II (KBo 51.15 and Bo 9628 are not included)

Obv. II

(Line numbers of Bo 9659 are in parentheses)

…

§ 8′ 18′ (= 1′) ^{LÚ}DAM.GÀR LỤ́-*i̯š* ^{d}UTỤ-*i kat-ta-an* GIŠ.RÍN

19′ (= 2′) *ḫar-zi nụ* GIŠ.RÍN *mar-šạ-nụ-uz-zi ú-gạ*

20′ (= 3′) *Ạ-NẠ* DINGIR-*YA ku-it i-i̯a-nu-   un*

---

§ 9′ 21′ (= 4′) *nu* É-*YA* ⸢*i*⸣*š-ḫa-aḫ-ru-*[*u̯*]*a-aš*[1)] É-*YA*

22′ (= 5′) ⸢*ki-i-ša*⸣- *ạt*

---

§ 10′ 23′ (= 6′) [*nu*(-)…] *pị́t-tụ-li-iš-ki-mi* ZI-*YA-p*[*át-ma*]

(Bo 9659 breaks here off; text continues in KUB 36.75 + Bo 9628 II 24′–25′)

Text-critical note: [1)] Differently from *pít-tu-li-i̯a-aš* in KUB 30.10 rev. 14, this reading follows a recent direct join with Bo 9628, and the whole sentence reads "*my house became my house of tea*[*r*]*s*."

Bo 9660

Description: Ritual.

CTH: 470 "*Fragments de rituels.*"

Dating and Script: NS.

Remarks: Small, one-sided fragment.

Measurements: 3.7 × 2.1 × 0.9 cm.

Bibliography: N/A.

Bo 9660

§ 1′ 1′]⌈*x-x*⌉[

2′]-*x̣-ma-x̣*(-)[

3′]-*x̣* KASKAL.MEŠ [[1)]

4′]-*x̣ im-mi-a*[*n-zi*$^{?}$

5′ *n*]*a-at pár-š*[*i-*

6′ *-i̯*]*a*$^{?}$*-na-az a-*[

7′]-*x̣ nu-u̯a*(-)[

8′] II$^{?}$-*an* [

(broken off)

Text-critical note: [1)] Perhaps belongs to the cultic phrase KASKAL.MEŠ *ḫuittiya-* "drawing paths," thus the text may be classified as a Kizzuwatnan / evocation ritual.

Bo 9661

Description: Ritual.

CTH: 470 "*Fragments de rituels.*"

Dating and Script: NS.

Remarks: Small, one-sided fragment.

Measurements: 2.7 × 4.5 × 1.2 cm.

Bibliography: N/A.

Bo 9661

§ 1′ 1′]-⸢*zi x*⸣(-)[
2′] *ṭi-i̯a-zi t*⸢*a-a*⸣[*n*(-)
3′ *me*]-⸤*ma*⸥-*aḫ-ḫi ka-a-aš* GẠL[1)](./-)[
4′ -*i̯*]*a-an-za nu i-da-a-l*[*a-*
5′ *al-u̯a-a*]*n-zé-na-aš* É-*i*[*r*(-)
6′]-*x̣*-⸤*ša ki-ịš*?⸥(-)[
(broken off)

Text-critical note: [1)] If the identification of the logogram is correct, "this cup" must refer to a *teššummi*-cup because of the common gender of the word, which is a part of an analogy spell given in lines 3′ ff.

Bo 9662

Description: Festival.

CTH: 645.8 "*Fragments de fêtes aux divinités de la terre.*"

Dating and Script: NS.

Remarks: Bo 9662 is a one-sided fragment whose lines 1′–8′ are duplicate or parallel to KUB 58.38 I 18′–25′ (NS). This fragment includes a list of deities similar to KUB 43.30 III 5′–8′ (OS), KBo 11.32 obv. 31–33 (NS), and KUB 58.38 I 11′–13′, 23′–25′.

Measurements: 3.4 × 2.1 × 1.5 cm.

Bibliography: Soysal, *Anatolica* 38, 186–87 (transliteration and remarks).

Bo 9662

§ 1′ 1′ [DUMU.MEŠ.É.G]⌈A⌉L [
2′ [LUGAL-*uš Q*]*A-TAM* *ḍ*[*a-a-i*
3′]-*x̣* *la-ḫ*[*u-u̯a*?*-an-zi*[1)]

---

§ 2′ 4′ [*ne-p*]*í-ša-aš* ^{d}[U-*aš kat-ti-iš-ši-ma*]
5′ [*an-na-a*]*š da-g*[*a-a-an-zi-pa-aš* ^{d}UTU-*uš*]
6′ [*kat-t*]*i-ị̇š-ši-mạ* [^{d}*Me-ez-zu-ul-la-aš*]
7′ [^{d}*Š*]*ụ-u̯ạ-li-i̯*[*a-az kat-ti-iš-ši-ma* ^{d}*Ḫal-ki-iš*]
8′ [^{d}*SÎN-aš*] ⌊*kat-ti*⌋-[*iš-ši-ma* ^{d}*Iš-pa-an-za-še-pa-aš*]
(broken off)

Text-critical note: [1)] For lines 1′–3′, see KUB 58.38 I 18′–21′: … DUMU.MEŠ.É.GAL IV ^{DUG}*KU-KU-UB*$^{\text{ḪI.A}}$ AN.BAR / [*a*]*-ap-pa-an-zi* LUGAL-*uš-kán QA-TAM da-a-i* / […]-*x̣-TIM* EGIR ^{GIŠ}ŠEN *ke-e-da-aš* / [… *la-a*?*-ḫ*]*u*?*-an-zi*.

Bo 9663

Description: Treaty$^{?}$.

CTH: 212 *"Traités (ou protocoles): fragments"* or 213 *"Fragments de listes divines (témoins)."*

Dating and Script: NS.

Remarks: Tiny, one-sided fragment, of which the preserved part contains only a list of deities$^{?}$.

Measurements: 3.8 × 3.2 × 2.1 cm.

Bibliography: N/A.

Bo 9663

§ 1′ 1′]-*x̣ zạ-a*⌈*p*$^{?}$*-x-x*⌉[1)][

---

§ 2′ 2′](-)*x̣*(-)*ịš*$^{?}$*-ḫ̮ạ-x̣-x̣-aš*$^{?}$ [2)] [

3′–4′ (traces)

5′ ^{UR}]^{U}*An-ku-u̯a-a*[*š* ^{d}*Ḫ̮a-tág-ga-aš*(?)[3)]

6′ ^{UR}]^{U}*Ša-m*[*u-ḫ̮a-aš* ^{d}*A-ba-ra-aš*(?)[4)]

7′](-)*x̣*(-)*tạ-*[5)] [

8′](-)*x̣*(-)*ḫ̮ụ-*[6)] [

(broken off)

Text-critical notes: [1)] Traces do not support a reading ^{d}*Za-ap-*(*pa-*)*na-aš* (KBo 50.48:6′, KBo 4.10+ rev. 1). [2)] To be read ^{d}*Ị̈š-ḫ̮ạ-rạ-ạ-aš* ? [3)] Cf. KBo 4.10+ rev. 2. [4)] Cf. KBo 4.10+ rev. 1. [5)] Or: [^{UR}]^{U}*Ta-*[…]. [6)] Or: [^{UR}]^{U}*Ḫ̮u-*[…].

Bo 9664

Description: N/A.

CTH: 832 "*Fragments en langue hittite de nature inconnue.*"

Dating and Script: N/A.

Remarks: One-sided fragment from the left and right columns of a tablet.

Measurements: 3.0 × 4.0 × 2.0 cm.

Bibliography: N/A.

Bo 9664 rev. III?

Left column (nothing preserved)

Right column (reverse III?)

§ 1′ 1′ Š⸢AḪ⸣(-)[

2′ *na-an-*⸢*kán*⸣ [

3′ *nu-u̯a-ra-a*[*š*

(bottom of the tablet)

Bo 9665 (+$^{?}$) KBo 35.102

Description: Ritual.

CTH: 490.1.A.6 "*Rituel de contre-magie*," which should be now labeled as "*Ritual of Ašdu.*"

Dating and Script: NS.

Remarks: This one-sided piece represents the top portion of a tablet including the upper edge. Bo 9665 lines 2–4 are duplicate to KUB 7.33+ obv. 2–6 (CTH 490.1.A.3; NS), KUB 60.159(+) obv. 1–3 (CTH 490.1.A.2; NS) and IBoT 4.27 obv. 1–5 (CTH 490.1.A.4; NS), from where the restorations are taken. Bo 9665 and KBo 35.102 (CTH 490.1.A.1; NS) may be pieces of the same tablet, but no confirmation is yet available.

Measurements: 2.0 × 5.1 × 2.5 cm.

Bibliography: Soysal, *Anatolica* 38, 184 (transliteration and remarks).

Bo 9665 obv. I

Left column (obverse I)

§ 1 1 [*UM-MA* ^{f}*A-aš-d*(*u* ^{MUNUS}ŠU.GI ^{URU}*Ḫur-l*)*a-aš*][1)]
2 [(*ma*)-*a-an al*-(*u̯a-an-za-aḫ-ḫa-an-da-an* UN-*an* EG)]IR-*pa* SIG$_5$-*aḫ-mi*
3 [(*na-an-kán ták-na-za*[2)] *da-aḫ-ḫi nu ki-i*)] ⌞*da-a*⌟*ḫ-ḫi*

---

§ 2 4 [(I DÀRA.MAŠ I GU$_4$ I UDU I TI$_8$^{MUŠEN} I SUR$_{14}$.DÙ.A^{MUŠEN} I *A*)]⌞*R-NA-B*⌟*U*[3)]
(broken off)

Text-critical notes: [1)] It is difficult to decide if this line is indeed inscribed as the first line of the ritual that I reconstruct here following the line order in IBoT 4.27 obv. 1–3. Otherwise, the line with SIG$_5$-*aḫ-mi* would have been extremely long for an introductory line; cf. Görke, *Aštu*, 34. [2)] IBoT 4.27 obv. 3: [*tá*]*k-na-az*. [3)] The order of the animal names in I 4, which ends with *ARNABU* "hare," permits the supposition that Bo 9665 and KBo 35.102 belong to the same tablet; thus, KBo 35.102 I 1′–4′ (+$^{?}$) Bo 9665 I 1–4.

Bo 9667

Description: Festival$^{?}$.

CTH: 670 "*Fragments divers*."

Dating and Script: ENS$^{?}$.

Remarks: One-sided fragment.

Measurements: 2.7 × 3.0 × 1.9 cm.

Bibliography: N/A.

Bo 9667

§ 1′ 1′](-)⌈*x̣-ú*$^{?}$(-)*x̣*⌉(-)[

2′] SILA$_4$-*an x̣*-[

3′] *ạ-še-eš-šar a*⌈*n-x*⌉[1)](-)[

4′ -*a*]*n-zi* SÍG-*ká*[*n*

5′]⌊*x-x-x*(-)*x-x*⌋[

(broken off)

Text-critical note: [1)] Or as a divine name ^{d}⌈*x*⌉(./-)[...].

Bo 9668

Description: N/A.

CTH: 832 “*Fragments en langue hittite de nature inconnue.*”

Dating and Script: NS.

Remarks: One-sided, lightly abraded fragment that is mostly illegible, hence hard to classify.

Measurements: 3.1 × 2.8 × 1.4 cm.

Bibliography: N/A.

Bo 9668

§ 1′ 1′–2′ (traces)

3′](-)*x̣*$^{?}$-*x̣*(-)*ạr*$^{?}$-[

4′ …

5′]-*x̣*$^{?}$-*x̣*(-) *x̣*(-) [

6′]-*x̣-aš*(-)*kạ*$^{?}$-*an-n*[*i*$^{?}$ (-)

7′]-*zị-lị*(?) *tạ*$^{?}$-*x̣*-[

8′]-*x̣-u̯a-aš* KUR-*YẠ*(-)[

9′](-)*x̣-ạt*$^{?}$-*rạ*$^{?}$-*aš* KUR-*ẹ*$^{?}$(-)[

10′ (traces)

(broken off)

Bo 9669

Description: Festival.

CTH: 670 "*Fragments divers.*"

Dating and Script: NS.

Remarks: One-sided fragment. The features of the festival described here refer to a text from the Hattian milieu.

Measurements: 2.6 × 3.5 × 0.7 cm.

Bibliography: N/A.

Bo 9669

§ 1′ 1′ *-z*]⸢*i*$^{?}$⸣ ^{KUŠ}*kur-*⸢*ša*⸣*-aš* [
2′ *-z*]⸢*i*$^{?}$⸣ $^{\text{LÚ.MEŠ}}$*ḫa-pí-aš* [
3′ *l*]*u-ú-li-aš še-er x̣-*[
4′ *A-ŠAR-Š*]*U-NU ap-pa-an-zi t*[*e ti-i*$^{?}$*-en-zi*[1)]
5′]-⸤*na*$^{?}$⸥*-aš* UGULA $^{\text{LÚ.}}$⸤^{MEŠ}*x*⸥-[
(broken off)

Text-critical note: [1)] Restoration follows KBo 20.26 + KBo 25.34 obv. 13′ (CTH 627.A), KBo 30.26+ rev. 5′ (CTH 649.II.a.1.1), and KBo 25.46:5′–6′ (CTH 649.I.8.A). Cf. also KBo 16.49+ I 11′–12′ (CTH 635.10), where the singular agent of the sentence is the king: LUGAL-*uš ú-iz-zi lu-ú-li-aš še-er A-ŠAR-Š*[*U e-ep-zi*] / *ta-aš ti-i-e-ez-zi* "The king comes, above the pool [he takes] hi[s] position and steps in."

Bo 9670

Description: N/A.

CTH: 832 "*Fragments en langue hittite de nature inconnue.*"

Dating and Script: NS.

Remarks: One-sided fragment that is too small to determine.

Measurements: 2.0 × 2.8 × 1.2 cm.

Bibliography: N/A.

Bo 9670

§ 1′	1′	]-*x̣* $^{\text{LÚ.MEŠ}}$K⌈AŠ$_4$⌉.[E(?)
	2′	](-)*x̣-a-ma-i*[1)] I$^?$ *x̣*(-)[
	3′	]-*ẹ*$^?$-*et-t*[*a*(-)
	4′	]⌊*x-x-x*⌋[
	(broken off)	

Text-critical note: [1)] [*t*]*a-a-ma-i* or [*d*]*a-a-ma-i* ? The first suggested spelling is not yet attested while the latter is found in KUB 55.63 II$^?$ 10′.

Bo 9671

Description: Festival.

CTH: 669 "*Grands fragments de fêtes.*"

Dating and Script: NS.

Remarks: Bo 9671 is a one-sided fragment whose rev. IV$^{?}$ lines 1′–9′ are duplicate to KBo 44.139 rev. IV 9′–17′ (CTH 669).

Measurements: 3.3 × 2.6 × 0.7 cm.

Bibliography: Roszkowska-Mutschler, DBH 22, 125–26 (to KBo 44.139).

Bo 9671 rev. V$^{?}$ and IV$^{?}$

Right column (reverse IV$^{?}$)

§ 1′ 1′ ⸢GIŠ⸣[(*ḫa-at-tal-u̯a-aš* GIŠ-*i* I-*ŠU*)]

2′ *na*[(*m-ma ḫa-aš-ši-i ta-pu-uš-za* I-*ŠU*)]

3′ *ši-i*⸢*p-p*⸣[(*a-an-ti*)[1)]]

---

§ 2′ 4′ LÚ.MEŠ $^{GIŠ!}$BANŠ[(UR GADA-*an ú-da*)-*an-zi*]

5′ *ta-aš-ta* [(NINDA.GUR$_4$.RA.ḪI.A *ka-r*)*i*$^{?}$-(*i̯*)*a*$^{?}$-*an-zi*]

6′ ^{LÚ}MUḪALDIM *ta̦*-[(*pí-ša-na-an* KUBB)AR]

7′ *da-a-i* [(*ta-aš-ta* NINDA.GUR$_4$.RA).Ḫ(I.A)]

8′ *p*⌞*í-r*⌟[(*a-an ar-ḫa* GUL-*zi*)]

9′ ⌞*n*⌟[(*am-ma ta-pí-ša-na-an* KUBBA)R]

(broken off)

Left column (reverse V$^{?}$)

§ 1′ 1′].⌜MEŠ$^{?}$⌝[2)]

2′–3′ …

4′ -*z*]*i*

(broken off)

Text-critical notes: [1)] KBo 44.139 IV 11′: *ši-pa-an-ti̦*. [2)] Or: […-*z*]⌜*i*⌝.

Bo 9673 + KBo 5.3

Description: Treaty.

CTH: 42.A "*Traité avec Hukkanna du Hayasa.*"

Dating and Script: Šupp. I/NS.

Remarks: Bo 9673 lines 1′–8′ directly join KBo 5.3 II 76–83 (NS). KBo 5.3 + Bo 9673 II 77–85 are duplicate to KUB 23.73 + KUB 26.37 + KBo 19.44a obv. 3′–9′ (NS), from where the restorations are taken.

Measurements: 3.2 × 2.6 × 0.9 cm.

Bibliography: Soysal, *Anatolica* 38, 170–72 (transliteration, translation, and commentary).

Bo 9673

Bo 9673 + KBo 5.3 obv. II (composite image)

Obverse II

(Line numbers of Bo 9673 are in parentheses)

§ 13 76 (= 1′)](-)*x̣ ku-u̯a-pí*

77 (= 2′) [(*IT-TI* ^{d})UTU-*ŠI*](-)⸢*x*$^{?}$-*x*⸣ *p̣ár*$^{?}$-*ki-i̯a-an-za-ma*

78 (= 3′) [*…-z*(*a*$^{?}$ *ku-u̯a-pí na-aš-šu-ma-k*)*án ku-u̯a-pí-i*(*k*)]-⸢*ki*⸣ *an-da pí-i-e-mi*

79 (= 4′) [… -(*x A-NA* KARAŠ *ku-u̯a-pí*)-*i*]*k-ki an-da pí-i-e-mi*[1)]

80 (= 5′) [(*i-d*)*a-a-lu-un me-mi-an*] *iš-ta-ma-aš-ti*

81 (= 6′) [(*na-an-mu ma-a-a*)*n Ú-UL ḫ*(*a-at-ra-a-ši z*)]*i-ig-ga-mu-uš-ša-an*

82 (= 7′) [(*lam*)-*ma*(*r Ú-UL*)] *a-ar-ti*

---

§ 14 83 (= 8′) [(*na-aš-ma-x*$^{?}$ *ŠA*$^{?}$) K(UR ^{URU}*Ḫa-i̯a-ša-ma nu i-d*)]*a-a-lu-ụn mẹ-mi-an*

84 (= 9′) [*iš-ta-ma-aš-ti* (*ku-i-ša-aš i*)]*m-ma k*[(*u-iš*)] *mẹ-mi-a*[(*š*)]

85 (= 10′) [(*nu-mu-uš-ša-an ma-a-an l*)*am-mar Ú-UL a-a*]⸤*r-t*⸥[*i* …]⸤*x*$^{?}$ *x*$^{?}$⸥[

(from here on Bo 9673 breaks off)

Text-critical note: [1)] Duplicate KBo 19.44a + obv. 5′: *pí-i̯a-mi*.

Bo 9674

Description: Ritual, cult inventory or festival.

CTH: 470 "*Fragments de rituels*," 530 or 670 "*Fragments divers*."

Dating and Script: NS.

Remarks: One-sided fragment from the right$^{?}$ column of a tablet.

Measurements: 3.0 × 2.9 × 1.1 cm.

Bibliography: N/A.

Bo 9674

§ 1′ 1′ ⸢*I-NA*(?) Ú.SAL(?)(-)*x̣*⸣(-)[

2′ ⸤*x̣*$^{?}$ N⸥INDA.GUR$_{4}$.RA GA.KỊN$^{?}$.[AG$^{?}$

3′ ⸤LÚ$^{?}$⸥ ^{d}U *PA-NI* ^{N}[^{A_4}ZI.KIN(?)

4′ [*IŠ-T*]*U*(?) II *š*[*u*-

5′ [DI]NGIR$^{?}$-*LUM-kán* ^{UR}[$^{U?}$

6′ EGIR-*an* *a*[*p*$^{?}$-

7′ EGIR-*ạn* *a*[*p*$^{?}$-

8′ ⸤*I-NA* *x-x̣*$^{?}$⸥(-)[

(broken off)

Bo 9675

Description: N/A.

CTH: 832 "*Fragments en langue hittite de nature inconnue.*"

Dating and Script: NS.

Remarks: Small, one-sided fragment from the right portion (with inscribed edge) of a tablet that cannot be classified.

Measurements: 3.3 × 1.2 × 2.3 cm.

Bibliography: N/A.

Bo 9675

Bo 9675 (right edge)

§ 1′ 1′ *-i̯*]⸢*a*? *x*⸣
2′ …
3′]-*x̣ pa-ra-a i-i̯a-a*[*n-*
4′ …
5′ *-n*]*a*? PAB?
6′ *-n*]*a*? *x-x-x*[1)]
7′]-*x̣-i̯ạ*
8′]-*x̣*
(broken off)

Text-critical note: [1)] The signs written on the tablet's edge seem to be distorted (or erased) rather than damaged.

Bo 9677

Description: Ritual$^{?}$.

CTH: 470 "*Fragments de rituels.*"

Dating and Script: NS.

Remarks: One-sided fragment from the left portion (with edge) of a tablet.

Measurements: 3.7 × 4.2 × 1.0 cm.

Bibliography: N/A.

Bo 9677

§ 1′ 1′ *x̣*-[

2′ *nu*(-)[

3′ *um*$^{?}$-*x̣*[1)]-[

4′ *da-r*⸢*a-an-du*$^{?}$⸣ [

5′ *ki-i-ma-u̯a* GI⸢Š⸣(./-)[

6′ *nu-za-kán* SAG.D⸢U⸣(./-)[

7′ *i̯-i̯a-an-ni-i̯a-zi̯* [

8′ ^{GIŠ}*tar-za-u*(?)-*an*[2)] *pa-ra-a x̣*-[

9′ *ti̯-i̯a̯-zi nu ú-i-x̣*-[

10′ [*ki-i*]*š̯-ša-an me-ma-i x̣*-[

11′ (traces)

(broken off)

Text-critical notes: [1)] *UM-M*[*A*] ? [2)] Despite a very clear script, it is hard to decide if this word is to be read ^{GIŠ}*nu-ḫa-an* (hence, a hapax) or ^{GIŠ}*tar-za-u-an* (a unique spelling for adjectival ^{GIŠ}*tar-zu-u̯a-a-an* "*tarzu*-furnished," as it appears in KUB 27.67+ II 12, III 17).

Bo 9678

Description: N/A.

CTH: 831 "*Fragments en langue inconnue ou indéterminée.*"

Dating and Script: N/A.

Remarks: One-sided fragment that is too small to classify.

Measurements: 4.0 × 4.9 × 1.6 cm.

Bibliography: N/A.

Bo 9678

§ 1′ 1′]-r⌈i-x-x?⌉(-)[

2′](-)x̣?(-)t⌊a-x⌋(-)[

3′]-⌈x⌉ [

4′](-)x̣-re-eš-š[a?(-)

5′ (-)i]n-na-x̣-[

6′ (traces)

(broken off)

Bo 9679 + KUB 10.72

Description: Festival.

CTH: 669.4.A "*Grands fragments de fêtes*."

Dating and Script: NS.

Remarks: Bo 9679 lines 1–7 directly join KUB 10.72 V 1–7 (NS). The lines of Bo 9679 are close to the left column divider, so that nothing is missing at the beginning of line 6.

Measurements: 3.5 × 3.2 × 1.1 cm.

Bibliography: Soysal, *Anatolica* 38, 187–88 (transliteration and translation).

Bo 9679

Bo 9679 + KUB 10.72 rev. V (composite image)

Reverse V

§ 1 1] ⸢É⸣.DINGIR-*LIM*-*K*[*A p*]*í-ra-an QA-TAM-MA*

2 [ÌR-*KA*[1)]] ⸢*e*⸣-*eš-du* ⸤*iš*?⸥-*ḫa-aš-šar-u-e-eš-du*

---

§ 2 3 [Í]D?<.MEŠ?>-*ma* GIM-*an ar-ša-an-zi*

4 [*z*]*i-ik-ka*$_4$-*ká*[*n*] DINGIR-*LUM* EN-*YA*

5 *Ạ-NA* É.DING⸤IR⸥-*LIM-KA* EGIR-*pa an-da-an*

6 *QA-TAM-MA ar-ši-i̯a-aḫ-ḫu-ut*

7 [*n*]⸤*u-za*⸥ *tu̯-el* É.DINGIR-*LIM-KA* ZAG.GAR.RA-*i̯a*

(Bo 9679 breaks here off; text continues in KUB 10.72 V 8 ff.)

Text-critical note: 1) There is space here for a maximum of two signs; for free restoration with ÌR-*KA*, cf. the context of KUB 10.72 V 9–11.

Bo 9680

Description: Ritual or festival?.

CTH: 470 "*Fragments de rituels*" or 670 "*Fragments divers.*"

Dating and Script: NS.

Remarks: Double-sided fragment.

Measurements: 4.5 × 3.6 × 2.0 cm.

Bibliography: N/A.

Bo 9680 obv.?

Bo 9680 rev.?

Bo 9680 rev.$^{?}$

Bo 9680 (right edge)

Obverse$^{?}$

§ 1′ 1′ *(-)p]a*$^{?}$*-an-x̣*(-)[...$^{?}$]

2′ Ì$^{?}$].UDU Ì.UZ$_6$$^{?}$ [1](-)[...$^{?}$]

3′]*-x̣-ta*

4′ ...

5′ *p]í*$^{?}$*-di*

6′ ...

(broken off)

Reverse$^{?}$

§ 1′ 1′]⸢*x x*⸣[

2′]-⸤*za*$^{?}$[2]⸥ *nu-u̯a-ra-aš-m*⸢*a*⸣-[*aš*$^{?}$]

3′ *-e*]*š*$^{?}$*-tén*

4′ KUŠ.SA]$_5$ KUŠ.BABBAR-*i̯a*[3] GAR-*ri*

5′](-)*x̣*[4]*-an-za*

---

§ 2′ 6′ LÚ.MEŠ(?)...]*-x̣*$^{?}$*-li-uš a-ša-an-*⸤*zi*$^{?}$⸥

7′]-⸤*x-m*⸥*a-aš-ma-aš*

8′]⸤*x*$^{?}$*-x-x*⸥[

(broken off)

Text-critical notes: [1] Reading is uncertain. For a similar shape of UZ$_6$ “goat,” see KBo 37.3 + rev. 6′. [2] Or: [...*-u*]⸤*n*⸥ as part of verbal ending in pret. sg. 1. [3] Cf. KBo 13.145 rev.$^{?}$ 9′, which likewise reads [KUŠ.S]A$_5$ KUŠ.BA̧BBAR-*i̯a*. [4] To be read [*t*]*i-* ?

Bo 9681

Description: Inventory, ritual, or festival[?].

CTH: 250 "*Fragments d'inventaires*," 470 "*Fragments de rituels,*" or 670 "*Fragments divers.*"

Dating and Script: N/A.

Remarks: One-sided fragment from the upper portion of a tablet (with edge) that is slightly abraded.

Measurements: 2.2 × 4.4 × 1.8 cm.

Bibliography: N/A.

Bo 9681

§ 1	1	](-)*x̣-x̣*[?]*-ri ŠA* GI *x̣*-[
	2	](-)*x̣-an kat-ta-ma x̣*-[
	3	*-i*]*š*[?]*-gur*[1)]*-ma-a*⌊*t*[?]⌋(-)[
§ 2	4	](-)*x̣-ną̣*[?] (-)[
		(broken off)

Text-critical note: [1)] Perhaps the word is to be completed as [*za-pí-i*]*š*[?]*-gur-*; cf. *za-pé-eš-gur* in KUB 42.39:5′ (to [(URUDU)]*zapiškur*(*i*)-, a metal implement).

Bo 9682

Description: Vow.

CTH: 590 "*Fragments de songes et d'ex-voto.*"

Dating and Script: NH/NS.

Remarks: One-sided fragment.

Measurements: 2.9 × 3.0 × 1.0 cm.

Bibliography: N/A.

Bo 9682

§ 1′ 1′]⌈*x-x-x*? *x-x x*⌉[

2′ *A-N*]*A* ^{d}*Ḫé-pát* ^{UR}[^{U} [1)]

3′] *ŠA* ^{d}UTU-*ŠI* SI[G$_{5}$?-

4′]-*x̣*(-)DINGIR-*LIM* I ZI ^{N}[$^{\mathrm{A4}}$ZA.GÌN(?)[2)]

5′ ALAM? *ŠA*?] ^{ḍ}*IŠTAR* GUŠKIN I GU[$_{4}$?(.)

6′]-*x̣ pí-iḫ-ḫi* ^{m}*Pí-ḫa*-⌊*x̣*⌋-[[3)]

7′ ALAM? *ŠA*?] ^{ḍ}*IŠTAR* GUŠKIN *x̣*-[

8′ *A-N*]*A* IN⌊IM?⌋(.)[

---

§ 2′ 9′ (traces)

(broken off)

Text-critical notes: [1)] Either ^{d}*Ḫé-pát* ^{UR}[^{U}*Kum-ma-an-ni*] (KUB 15.29 I 3′, 9′, 14′; CTH 590) or ^{d}*Ḫé-pát* ^{UR}[^{U}*U-da*] (KUB 15.1 I 1, 4, 14; CTH 584). [2)] Cf. KBo 55.208 rev.? 15′ (CTH 584). [3)] Most likely to be identified as ^{m}*Piḫa*-^{d}U. For the frequent mention of this person in votive texts, see de Roos, *Votive*, 68 f.

Bo 9683

Description: N/A.

CTH: 832 "*Fragments en langue hittite de nature inconnue.*"

Dating and Script: NS$^{?}$.

Remarks: One-sided fragment.

Measurements: 3.1 × 3.2 × 1.6 cm.

Bibliography: N/A.

Bo 9683

§ 1′	1′	](-)*x̣*$^{?}$-*ạ-a*[*n*(-)
	2′	-*n*]*a*$^{?}$-*u-u̯a-x̣*$^{?}$(-)[
	3′	*Ú-UL*(?)] *ka-ni-ẹ*$^{?}$-[*eš*$^{?}$-*zi*$^{?}$ [1]
	4′	-*i̯*]*a*$^{?}$-*na-aš Ú-U*[*L ka-ni-e-eš-zi*(?)]
	5′	](-)⸤*x̣* *x̣*⸥ *Ú-U*[*L ka-ni-e-eš-zi*(?)]
	6′	]⸤*x x x x*⸥[
	(broken off)	

Text-critical note: [1] Cf. KUB 48.109(+) II 3′: [*Ú-U*]*L ka-ni-ẹ*-[*eš-zi*] and the following lines 4′–10′ with repetitive *ka-ni-e-eš-zi*. If the restorations for Bo 9683:3′–5′ are correct, this fragment may belong to the composition of KUB 48.109 (+) KBo 22.178 (CTH 457.7.2).

Bo 9686

Description: N/A.

CTH: 831 "*Fragments en langue inconnue ou indéterminée.*"

Dating and Script: (L)NS.

Remarks: One-sided fragment that is possibly not in Hittite.

Measurements: 2.7 × 2.1 × 1.5 cm.

Bibliography: N/A.

Bo 9686

§ 1′ 1′]-*lụ*-⸢*ga-an-x̣*⸣[1)](-)[
2′] *a-at-ru*(-)[[2)]
3′ -*n*]*u-uš* [
4′]-*li-i̯a* (-)*x̣*(-)[
5′]-*x̣-ru-uš a-x̣*-[
6′ -*š*]*a*[?] [
7′](-)⸤*x̣*[?]-*x-ị*[?]-*x*⸥(-)[
(broken off)

Text-critical notes: [1)] If the text is written in Hittite, this is probably to be restored as [^{GIŠ}*ḫu*]-*lụ*-⸢*ga-an-n*⸣[*i*[?](-)...[?]].
[2)] This initial part of a word does not fit any lemma from the ancient Anatolian languages known to date.

Bo 9688

Description: Festival.
CTH: 670 "*Fragments divers.*"
Dating and Script: NS.
Remarks: One-sided fragment.
Measurements: 3.2 × 2.4 × 1.8 cm.
Bibliography: N/A.

Bo 9688

§ 1′ 1′]⌈*x-x*⌉[
2′ ^{GI}]$^{\text{Š?}}$*ẓa-ḫur-ti* Ẹ́$^{?}$.[
3′ UD]U$^{?}$ *I-NA* Ẹ́.[
4′ ^{GIŠ}BANŠUR$^{?}$] ⌊A⌋D.KID $^{\text{LÚ.MEŠ}}$*x̣*-[

---

§ 2′ 5′ L]UGAL$^{?}$ *A-N*[*A*$^{?}$
6′ (-)*u*]*š*$^{?}$-*x̣*-[
7′]⌊*x*⌋[
(broken off)

Bo 9689

Description: Letter$^?$.

CTH: 210 "*Varia.*"

Dating and Script: (E)NH$^?$.

Remarks: Double-sided fragment with inscribed upper edge.

Measurements: 3.1 × 4.2 × 1.8 cm.

Bibliography: N/A.

Bo 9689 (upper edge)

Bo 9689 obv.

Bo 9689 rev.

Upper edge

§ 1 1 ⌊XVII$^{?}$⌋ ^{UDU}*i-i̯a-an-t*⌊*a*⌋-[*aš*$^{?}$

Obverse

2 *ẋ-ẋ$^{?}$-at-ta$^{?}$-an* *ẋ*-[

3 *zị-ịk-u̯a-az* *ẋ*-[

4 BURU$_{14}$-*ma-u̯a-az* *t*[*a*$^{?}$-

5 *nu-uš-šị-kán* SỊ́G(./-)*ẋ*(-)[

6 ⌊*nu-uš*⌋-[*š*]⌊*i-kán* *ẋ*⌋(-)[

(broken off)

Reverse

§ 1′ 1′ ⸢*a*$^{?}$⸣-[

2′ *pa-ra-*⸢*a*⸣ [

(bottom of the tablet)

Bo 9691

Description: Festival.

CTH: 670 "*Fragments divers.*"

Dating and Script: NS.

Remarks: One-sided fragment.

Measurements: 3.9 × 2.6 × 1.5 cm.

Bibliography: N/A.

Bo 9691

§ 1′ 1′ …

---

§ 2′ 2′ I$^{?}$ ^{NINDA}*ta-kar-mu*]-*ụ́-ụn*[1] [
3′ -*n*]*i*$^{?}$[2] *pár-ši-i̯*[*a*

---

§ 3′ 4′ ^{d}… ^{d}…]-*x*-*šu-na*[3] TUŠ-*a*[*š*
5′]-*x* EGIR-*ŠÚ* ^{d}*x*-[

---

§ 4′ 6′ *IŠ-TU*(?) G]ẠL[4] I-Š[*U*
7′ -*i̯*]*a*$^{?}$
(broken off)

Text-critical notes: [1] The verb *paršiya-* "to break" in the following line would suggest a bread designation here rather than a divine name such as [^{d}…]-*ụ́-ụn*. [2] To be restored [*A-NA* ^{d}IŠKUR/U-*n*]*i* ? Cf. KBo 20.63 I 14–15 (CTH 630.B). [3] Either an independent divine name [^{d}…]*šuna* or inflected [^{d}…]*šun*(acc.)=*a*. [4] So, rather than [T]UŠ-*aš*, for which see line 4′.

Bo 9692

Description: Ritual or festival.

CTH: 470 "*Fragments de rituels*" or 670 "*Fragments divers.*"

Dating and Script: NS.

Remarks: One-sided fragment from the top portion (with edge) of a tablet.

Measurements: 3.2 × 2.3 × 2.2 cm.

Bibliography: N/A.

Bo 9692

Left column[1)]

§ 1 1]-*ị̣z-zi*

2]-*an-zi x̣*-[

Right column

§ 1 1–2 (written as continuation of the left column)

---

§ 2 3 TÚG *ka*-[

4 I TÚG *x̣*(.*/*-)[

5 ⌊*mu*?⌋-[

(broken off)

Text-critical note: [1)] If this column after the line 2 is uninscribed, then it could be rev. IV (with colophon ?).

Bo 9693

Description: Ritual or festival?.

CTH: 470 "*Fragments de rituels*" or 670 "*Fragments divers*."

Dating and Script: NS.

Remarks: One-sided fragment.

Measurements: 2.9 × 2.7 × 1.5 cm.

Bibliography: N/A.

Bo 9693

§ 1′ …

---

§ 2′ 1′ -i̯]a? x̣-[

2′] DINGIR.MEŠ Ẹ́?(.)[

3′]-x̣ *IŠ-TU* SÍ[G.

4′]-x̣-*kán A-NA* x̣-[

5′] *x* (erased?) [

(bottom of the tablet)

Bo 9695

Description: Ritual or festival.

CTH: 470 “*Fragments de rituels*” or 670 “*Fragments divers*.”

Dating and Script: NS.

Remarks: One-sided fragment; the right column is seemingly written with a smaller script than the left one.

Measurements: 2.7 × 3.6 × 1.9 cm.

Bibliography: N/A.

Bo 9695

Left column

§ 1′ 1′]-⸢*ḫa*?⸣
2′–3′ …
4′ -*t*]*i*?
5′](-)*ạ-ri*
(broken off)

Right column

§ 1′ 1′ *na-ạt-kán* [
2′ GIŠ*ḫa-aḫ*!*-ri-mạ*(-)[1)][

---

§ 2′ 3′ ẸGIR-*ŠÚ-m*⸤*a*?⸥[
4′ *ạn-d*[*a*?(-)
(broken off)

Text-critical note: [1)] Thus, sg. dat.-loc. to GIŠ*ḫaḫ*(*ḫa*)*ra-* “rake?” and not *GIŠ*za-aḫ-ri-* to GIŠ*zaḫrai-* (a wooden object), as the signs would rather indicate.

Bo 9696

Description: Ritual or festival.

CTH: 470 "*Fragments de rituels*" or 670 "*Fragments divers.*"

Dating and Script: NS.

Remarks: One-sided fragment from the left portion (with edge) of a tablet. The line order including the repetitive EGIR-*ŠÚ-ma* reminds one of the Kizzuwatnan festivals with Hurrian divinities who receive offerings, but also KUB 4.1 IV 34′–42′ (CTH 422.A), a list of dance steps.

Measurements: 3.2 × 2.4 × 2.5 cm.

Bibliography: N/A.

Bo 9696

§ 1′ 1′ LÚ.⸢ME⸣[Š [1)]

---

§ 2′ 2′ EGIR-*ŠÚ-ma* [

---

§ 3′ 3′ EGIR-*ŠÚ-ma t*[*u*-[2)]

---

§ 4′ 4′ EGIR-*ŠÚ-ma* [

---

§ 5′ 5′ EGIR-*ŠÚ-m*[*a*

(broken off)

Text-critical notes: [1)] LÚ.ME[ŠḪUB.BÍ] ? Cf. KUB 4.1 IV left side 32′. [2)] Either to Hurrian divinities like *tu-u-ni tap-ri* etc. (KUB 25.44 II? 4′ [CTH 704.5.A], KUB 27.8 rev.? 7 [CTH 704.2.A]), or to the dance-step descriptions starting with the word *tu-u-az*(*-za*), *tu-u-u̯a-az/za* "far apart" (KUB 4.1 IV left side 35′, 36′, 41′, 42′, right side 32′, 34′, 36′).

Bo 9697

Description: Festival.
CTH: 670 "*Fragments divers.*"
Dating and Script: NS.
Remarks: One-sided fragment.
Measurements: 3.5 × 3.1 × 1.0 cm.
Bibliography: N/A.

Bo 9697

§ 1′ 1′ *-i̯]ạ-z[i*

---

§ 2′ 2′ *]-x̣ ma-aḫ-ḫa-*⌈*a*⌉[*n*(-)
3′ *a*$^{?}$*-r]a-an-zi nu* ^{L}[$^{\text{Ú.MEŠ}}$
4′ *kat-t]a-an*[1)] *pár-a*⌊*š-na*⌋-[*a*$^{?}$*-an-zi*

---

§ 3′ 5′ *]-x̣-ši-kán x̣-*[
6′]⌊*x x*⌋[
(broken off)

Text-critical note: [1)] Cf. KUB 11.24(+) VI 15.

Bo 9698 + KUB 23.13

Description: Historical.

CTH: 211.4 "*Fragments historiques. Annales.*"

Dating and Script: NH/NS.

Remarks: Bo 9698 is a one-sided fragment whose lines 1–3 join directly to KUB 23.13:9–11 (NS).

Measurements: 3.4 × 2.9 × 1.7 cm.

Bibliography: Soysal, *Anatolica* 38, 174–77 (transliteration, translation, and commentary).

Bo 9698

Bo 9698 (right edge)

Bo 9698 + KUB 23.13 (composite image)

(Line numbers of Bo 9698 are in parentheses)

§ 1 9 (= 1)]-*x̣ ar-nu-nu-un na-an* ^{URU}PÚ-*na* ^{d}UTU-*aš* URU-*ri ú-u̯a-te-nu-un*

---

§ 2 10 (= 2) ^{m}*La-b*]*a-ar-na* LUGAL.[G]AL KUR-TU_4 *U*⌞*L pa-i*⌟*t nu* NUMUN ^{m}*Mu̥-ú-a*-UR.MAḪ

11 (= 3) -*Y*]*A*?[1)] *i-i̯a-nu-un* [*n*]*u-u̥š-ši-kán* K[ARA]Š? ANŠE.KUR.RA *ša-ra-a*

12 (= 4) [*u-i-i̯a-nu-un*(?)]

---

§ 3 13 (= 5)]-⌞*x̣-an*⌟-[*n*]*e-i̯ạ-ạt-tạ-ạt*?

14 (= 6)]-⌞*k*⌟*án* LỤGAL ^{KUR}*Ạḫ̮*-[*ḫ*]*i-i̯ạ-u̥*-[*u̯a*(-)...?]

15 (= 7)]-*x̣* [

(broken off)

Text-critical note: [1)] The broken sign is hard to identify: possibly either an "*un*" or "*i̯a*."

Bo 9699

Description: Historical.

CTH: 215 “*Fragments non caractérisés.*”

Dating and Script: MS.

Remarks: One-sided fragment. As regards ductus and content, Bo 9699 is strongly reminiscent of the Middle Hittite fragment KBo 50.4 (CTH 148); thus, they are possibly pieces of the same tablet.

Measurements: 2.4 × 3.3 × 1.2 cm.

Bibliography: N/A.

Bo 9699

§ 1′ 1′]⸢*x̣ x̣ x̣ x̣*$^{?}$⸣[
2′]-*x̣-na* URU-*a*[*n*[1)]
3″ …$^{?}$

---

§ 2′ 4″](-)*x̣-UT-TI-ŠU*[2)] EG[IR$^{?}$(-)
5″]-*ẹš*$^{?}$*-ki-ir nam-ma*(-)[
6″]-*x̣-i̯ạ-aš* ^{URU}KÙ.BẠBBAR$^{?}$(-)*x̣*$^{?}$(-)[
7″]⸤*x̣ x̣ x̣ x̣*⸥[
(broken off)

Text-critical notes: [1)] This line can be alternatively read as […] *Ạ-NA* ^{URU}*A*[*n-*…] or ^{URU}*Ḫal-*[…] or even URU.DIDLI.[ḪI.A]. [2)] Perhaps [… *A-MI*]-*LỤ*$^{?}$*-UT-TI-ŠU* “[to / of] its [pe]ople.”

Bo 9700

Description: Instruction$^{?}$.

CTH: 275 "*Fragments de protocoles (ou de traités ?).*"

Dating and Script: LNS.

Remarks: One-sided fragment; a space for ca. 6 lines seems to be blank.

Measurements: 4.4 × 3.0 × 1.7 cm.

Bibliography: N/A.

Bo 9700

§ 1′ 1′ Š]*A*$^{?}$ DINGIR-*LIM-ma* *x̣*$^{?}$-[

2′]-*x̣*[2)] *na-aš-mạ-a*[*š*$^{?}$(-)

3′]-*x̣-te-ni* [

---

§ 2′ 4′ *ku-i-e*]-*ẹš* $^{LÚ.M}$[^{EŠ} [3)]

(broken off)

Text-critical notes: [1)] The sign looks like the end of a "*nu*," thus [...-*KU-N*]*U* ? [2)] One would expect for this line the phrase [*anda*=*ma*=*za šumeš* / *šumaš kui*]*eš* $^{LÚ.M}$[^{EŠ}...]; cf. KUB 13.3(+) III 3, 9 (CTH 265.1), KUB 13.4 II 52′, 73′, III 55, IV 34 (CTH 264.A), etc.

Bo 9701

Description: Ritual or festival.

CTH: 470 "*Fragments de rituels*" or 670 "*Fragments divers.*"

Dating and Script: NS.

Remarks: One-sided fragment.

Measurements: 4.3 × 2.5 × 1.1 cm.

Bibliography: N/A.

Bo 9701

§	Line	Text
§ 1′	1′	^{GIŠ}]PẠN(?)(./-)[
	2′	](-)*x̣-aš* I$^{?}$ *x̣*$^{?}$(.)[
	3′	GA.KIN].ẠG *pár-šu-l*[*a*$^{?}$-
§ 2′	4′	*p*]*a-ịz-zi nu-u*⌈*š*$^{?}$*-k*⌉[*án*$^{?}$
	5′	*-r*]*a*$^{?}$*-ma-aš-ša-an* Ị$^{?}$ [
	6′	SÍG$^{?}$.S]A$_5$ *ar-ḫa dạ-*[*a*$^{?}$*-i*$^{?}$
	7′	]-*x̣* *nu* *ki-*[
§ 3′	8′	](.)SAG-*az ḫ*[*a*-
	9′	](.)⌊x⌋.ḪỊ.A *n*[*a*$^{?}$-
	10′	]⌊*x̣*⌋[

(broken off)

Bo 9702

Description: Cult inventory or festival.

CTH: 530 or 670 "*Fragments divers.*"

Dating and Script: NH/NS.

Remarks: One-sided fragment.

Measurements: 2.9 × 3.2 × 1.2 cm.

Bibliography: N/A.

Bo 9702

§ 1′ 1′ (traces)

2′ *A-NA* ^{d}… ^{UR}]^{U}*An-ku-*⌈*u̯*⌉*a* ⌈BAL-*an-zi*⌉[1] [

3′ *šu-up-p*]*a* *ḫu-u-e-ša*[2]*-u̯a-az* [

4′]⌊I?⌋ PA ZÍD.DA I ^{DUG}KA.D[Ù[3]

5′ I P]⌊A Z⌋ÍD.DA I ^{DUG}KA.[DÙ[4]

6′ I D]UG.KAŠ ^{GIŠ}ZA⌊G.G⌋[AR.RA-*ni*[5]

7′ N]INDA.GUR$_4$.R[A(./-)

(broken off)

Text-critical notes: [1] Thus, rather than ⌈*ti-an-zi*⌉; cf. KBo 2.4 III 12′–13′ (CTH 672.D). [2] The sign "*ša*" exhibits here a unique shape. [3-4] To be restored with *aš-ša-nu-um-ma-aš* ? Cf. KBo 2.13 obv. 17 (CTH 505.2). [5] Cf. KBo 2.13 obv. 16.

Bo 9704

Description: Festival.

CTH: 670 "*Fragments divers.*"

Dating and Script: ENS$^{?}$.

Remarks: One-sided fragment. The mention of the profession ^{LÚ}*taḫiyala-* (lines 7′, 9′) suggests a festival from the Hattian cult milieu.

Measurements: 4.2 × 2.4 × 1.5 cm.

Bibliography: N/A.

Bo 9704

§ 1′ 1′ …

———

§ 2′ 2′ GIŠ] ⸢^{d}INA⸣NNA.G[AL

3′ GIŠ ^{d}]INANNA.GAL GI[Š$^{?}$

4′]-*zi* GIŠ ^{ḍ}[INANNA.GAL$^{?}$

———

§ 3′ 5′]-*x̣-aš*$^{?}$ ^{LÚ}SANGA $^{\text{d?}}$[

6′] ^{ḍ}*Ka-am-ma-m*[*a*(-)

7′ $^{\text{LÚ.MEŠ}}$*t*]*a*$^{?}$ [1]-*ḫi-i̯a-le-e*[*š*(-)

———

§ 4′ 8′ ^{d}…]-*x̣-i̯a-an* GU[B-*aš*(?)

9′ $^{\text{LÚ.MEŠ}}$*ta*$^{?}$ [2)]-⸤*ḫi-i̯*⸥*a-le-e*[*š*(-)

———

§ 5′ 10′]-*x̣-an x̣*-[

11′]-*x̣-d*[*u*$^{?}$-

(broken off)

Text-critical notes: [1-2)] Or to be read $^{\text{LÚ.MEŠ}}$*da-ḫi-i̯a-le-eš* ?

Bo 9705

Description: Ritual or vow$^{?}$.

CTH: 470 "*Fragments de rituels*" or 590 "*Fragments de songes et d'ex-voto.*"

Dating and Script: NS.

Remarks: One-sided fragment.

Measurements: 4.2 × 2.7 × 0.9 cm.

Bibliography: N/A.

Bo 9705

§ 1′ 1′] LỤGAL(-)[
2′]-x̣ LUGAL-x̣(-)[
3′ KUBBA]BAR$^{?}$ GUŠKIN [
4′ *-d*]*ụ*$^{?}$*-i̯a-u̯a-m*[*a*$^{?}$(-)
5′]-*x̣* [
6′]-*x̣-at ku-it*(-)*x̣*$^{1)}$(-)[

---

§ 2′ 7′]-*x̣-iš* GUNNI [...$^{?}$]
8′] *ị-i̯a-mi* [
(broken off)

Text-critical note: $^{1)}$ This sign is unlikely to be "*u̯a*"; cf. the form in line 4′.

Bo 9706

Description: Ritual or festival.

CTH: 470 "*Fragments de rituels*" or 670 "*Fragments divers.*"

Dating and Script: NS.

Remarks: One-sided fragment.

Measurements: 2.6 × 3.4 × 0.9 cm.

Bibliography: N/A.

Bo 9706

§ 1′	1′	](-)⸢*ú*?-*x*⸣-[
	2′	]-*x̣* DINGIR-*LIM*-*ni* ⸢*a*?⸣-[[1]
	3′	] *e-ep-zi* [2][
§ 2′	4′	]-*x̣*-*zạ*? *nam-ma* x̣.A(?)[3] *A-N*[*A*(?)
§ 3′	5′	(-)*d*]*a*?-*an-zi* ŠÀ *x̣*(./-)[
§ 4′	6′	]-⸤*at-ša*(?)⸥(-)[
	(broken off)	

Text-critical notes: [1] Based on the sign remnants maybe to be read and restored as [LUGAL-*u*]*š* DINGIR-*LIM*-*ni* ⸢*a*⸣-[*ru-u̯a-a-iz-zi*]; cf. KBo 8.117 II 8′. [2] [*A-ŠAR-ŠU*] *e-ep-zi* ? Cf. KBo 8.117 II 7′. [3] This word consisting of two signs could be a logogram.

Bo 9708 + KBo 15.14 + KUB 36.94

Description: Ritual.

CTH: 419.G "*Rituel de substitution royale.*"

Dating and Script: NS.

Remarks: Bo 9708 is a one-sided fragment whose lines 1′–6′ are duplicate to KUB 24.5 + KUB 9.13 + FHL 125 obv. 31′–35′, rev. 1–2 (CTH 419.A; LNS) and KUB 36.93 rev. 1′–7′ (CTH 419.C; NS), from where the restorations are taken. My early suggestion that if Bo 9708 (NS) and KBo 15.14 + KUB 36.94 (CTH 419.G; NS) were pieces of the same tablet, then KBo 15.14 + 1′–5′ may follow Bo 9708:2′–6′ after a brief gap of ca. 2–3 signs, has not been fully confirmed after a physical examination of both fragments by İ. Aykut (personal communication; see Soysal, *Anatolica* 38, 183). Meanwhile, F. Fuscagni claimed again the possible join Bo 9708 + KBo 15.14 (see the link below). In December 2012, I was able to check both pieces in Ankara myself. Despite the fact that they have no contact on their surface, and KBo 15.14 shows a different, totally blackened, color from Bo 9708, they have, however, a clear point of contact in the internal part of the tablet so that they could be glued together, as seen in the photo on the following page.

Measurements: 2.8 × 2.9 × 1.8 cm.

Bibliography: Soysal, *Anatolica* 38, 183–84 (transliteration and remarks); *Konkordanz*, http://www.hethport.uni-wuerzburg.de/hetskiz/sk.php?f=508/u.

Bo 9708

Bo 9708 + KBo 15.14 (KUB 36.94 not shown)

Bo 9708 + KBo 15.14 (composite image; KUB 36.94 not shown)

Reverse

(Line numbers of KBo 15.14 + KUB 36.94 are in parentheses)

§ 1′ 1′ (*ši-pa-an-t*)]*i*

---

§ 2′ 2′ (= 1′) (^{d}UTU A)]N-*E* E[(N-*YA*) *ku*]-⸢*it ku-it*⸣ [

3′ (= 2′) (*i-ši-i̯a-aḫ-t*)]*a* *nu-u̯a* [(*k*)*a*-(*a-š*)]*a am-mu-uk A-N*[*A*[1]

4′ (= 3′)] *a̦-pu-u-u*[*š*[2] *da-a*]*t-tén am-mu-uk-ma* [

5′ (= 4′) ^{d}UT(U ^{URU}*A-ri-in-n*)]*a* *ú-u̯*[(*a-an-n*)]*a* *ḫa̦-ši-ig-gal-lu*[3] [

6′ (= 5′) (*A-N*)]*A* ^{d}⸤E⸥[(REŠ.KI.GAL IV?[4] UD)]U.NÍTA BAL-*an-ti*[5] [

(Bo 9708 breaks off here; text continues in KBo 15.14 + KUB 36.94 rev. 6′ ff.)

Text-critical notes: [1] KUB 24.5 + KUB 9.13 + FHL 125 obv. 33′ omits *A-NA*. [2] Thus, revise the restoration [*ku-u-uš*] once suggested by Kümmel, StBoT 3, 10, for KUB 24.5+ obv. 34′. [3] This verbal form varies in KUB 24.5+ rev. 1: *ḫa-aš-ši-*⸢*ik-lu*⸥ and in KUB 36.93 rev. 6′: *ḫa̦-aš-ši-ig-ga̦l-lu.* [4] The sign partially preserved only in FHL 125+ rev. 2 appears to be higher than the number “I.” [5] KUB 24.5+ rev. 2: *š*[*i-pa-an*]⸢ ⸥*-ti.*

Bo 9710

Description: Ritual or festival.

CTH: 470 "*Fragments de rituels*" or 670 "*Fragments divers.*"

Dating and Script: NS.

Remarks: One-sided tablet fragment including the colophon.

Measurements: 4.1 × 4.2 × 1.7 cm.

Bibliography: N/A.

Bo 9710 rev. IV?

Reverse IV?

§ 1′ 1′]⌈*Ú-U*⌉[*L*(-)[1]

2′ U$_4$.XI.KAM[2] *t*]*úḫ-ḫu-u*[*š-ta*[3]

Colophon

§ 2′ 3′ DUB].*x*.KAM *ŠA* U$_4$.XI.KA[M

4′ (illegible traces)

(broken off)

Text-critical notes: [1] Cf. KBo 24.110 (+) KBo 23.49 IV 9′ (CTH 652.II.A): *ma-a-an Ú-UL-aš* [*t*]*a*?*-pa a-ap-pa-i* U$_4$.VIII.KAM *túḫ-ḫu-uš-ta*. [2] Restoration is based on the information in the colophon. [3] For *tuḫḫuš-* "to come to an end" immediately before the tablet's colophon, see KBo 14.84 IV 5′–7′, KBo 23.64 III 16′–17′, KBo 24.110 (+) KBo 23.49 IV 16′–17′, KUB 30.18 + KUB 39.3 IV 11′–15′, KUB 48.112 IV 10′–11′.

Bo 9711

Description: N/A.

CTH: 832 "*Fragments en langue hittite de nature inconnue.*"

Dating and Script: NS.

Remarks: One-sided fragment that is too small to classify.

Measurements: 3.0 × 3.7 × 1.2 cm.

Bibliography: N/A.

Bo 9711

§ 1′	1′	]⌈*x*⌉[
	2′	*ka*]*r*?-*pí*-*i*[*n*(-)
	3′	]-*x̣* [
	4′	-*z*]*i* [
§ 2′	5′	]-*x̣*-*zi* [
	6′	-*a*]*n*? *e*-*e*[*p*-*zi*]
	7′	]⌊*x*-*x*⌋[

(broken off)

Bo 9712 + KUB 9.32

Description: Ritual.

CTH: 394.C "*Rituel d'Ashella, contre une épidémie dans l'armée.*"

Dating and Script: MH/NS.

Remarks: This is a piece from the missing right edge of KUB 9.32 obv. 25 ff. (NS). A direct join is realized through the word *pidanzi* in the end of obv. 25 on the right edge. Bo 9712 + KUB 9.32 obv. 25–35 are duplicate to KUB 9.31 III 44–59, HT 1 III 37–44, KUB 41.17 III 1′–8′, KBo 13.212:1′–5′ (all NS), from where the restorations are taken.

Measurements: 5.3 × 2.4 × 2.2 cm.

Bibliography: Soysal, *Anatolica* 38, 180–82 (transliteration and remarks); *Konkordanz*, http://www.hethport.uni-wuerzburg.de/hetskiz/sk.php?f=Bo%202038.

Bo 9712

Bo 9712 (right edge)

Bo 9712 + KUB 9.32 obv. (composite image)

Obverse

(Line numbers of Bo 9712 are in parentheses)

…

§ 4 25 (= 1′) *nam-ma-kán* UDU.ŠIR.ḪI.A[1] MUNUS-*TU*$_4$-*i̯a*[2] NINDA.GUR$_4$.RA KAŠ-*i̯a* KẠRAŠ[3] *iš-tar-na ar-ḫa* ⌊*pí*[4]-*d*⌋*ạ-ạn-zị*

26 (= 2′) *na-aš* LÍL-*ri pé-en-na*[5]-*an-zi na-aš-kán pa-a-an-zi A-NA*[6] ZAG [LÚ]KÚR *an-dạ*

27 (= 3′) *ar-ḫa pí-it-ta*[7]-*la-an-zi ku-e-da-nị pí-dị an-ze-el Ú-UL a-ra-an-*[(*z*)]*i*[8]

28 (= 4′) *nu-kán an-da QA-TAM-MA-pát me-mi-iš-kán-zi ka-a-ša-u̯a-aš-ša-an ku-i*[(*t*)[9]]

29 (= 5′) *i-da-a-lu A-NA A-MI-LU-UT-TI* GUD.ḪI.A UDU.ḪI.A ANŠE.KUR.RA.MEŠ ANŠE.GÌR.NUN.N[(A).MEŠ[10]]

30 (= 6′) *Ụ A-NA* ANŠE.MEŠ[11] *ku-it*[12] *an-da e-eš-ta ki-nu-na-u̯a-ra-at-kán ka-a-š*[(*a*)[13]]

31 (= 7′) *IŠ-TU* KARAŠ *ku-u-uš* UDU.ŠIR.ḪI.A[14] MUNUS-*TU*$_4$[15] *ar-ḫa ú-te-er*

32 (= 8′) *nu-u̯a-ra-aš*[16]-*za ku-iš ú-e-mi-i̯a*[17]-*zi nu-u̯a-za ki-i* ḪUL[18] ⌈ÚŠ⌉-*an a-pa-*[(*a-aš* KUR)[19]]-⌈*ẹ-a*⌉*n-za da-a-ú*

---

§ 5 33 (= 9′) *I-NA* UD.II.KAM *ma-a-an lu-uk-kat-ta ka-ri-u̯a-a-ri-u̯a-ar*[20] *ḫu*[21]-*d*[(*a-ak* VI UDU)].⌊Š⌋IR[22] VI MÁŠ.GA[(L)[23]]

34 (= 10′) XII [DUG]GÌR.KÁN XỊI GAL.ḪI.A[24] XII NINDA.GUR$_4$.RA I [DUG]*ḫu*[25]-*up-pár* KAŠ III GỊR.T[(UR ZABA)]R[26] *ḫạ-ạn-dạ-ạn-z*[(*i*)[27]]

35 (= 11′) *na-aš* LÍL-*ri nam-ma da*[28]-*me-e-da-ni AŠ-RI pé-en-na*[29]-*an-zi k*[(*i-i-i̯a*[30] *ḫu-u-m*)]⌊*a*⌋-[(*an*)[31]]

…

(text continues in KUB 9.32 obv. 36 ff.)

Text-critical notes: [1] Mistakenly transliterated as UDU.ŠIR-*aš*[ḪI.A] by Dinçol, *Belleten* XLIX/193, 15. The supposed "*aš*" is in fact part of the sign "ŠIR." [2] KUB 9.31 III 44: MUNUS-*an*. [3] KUB 9.31 III 44: *A-NA* KARAŠ. [4] KUB 9.31 III 45 and HT 1 III 39: *pé-e-*. [5] KUB 9.31 III 45 and HT 1 III 40: *pé-en-ni-*. [6] HT 1 III 40: omits *A-NA*. [7] KUB 9.31 III 46: *pít-ta-*; HT 1 III 41: *píd-da-*. [8] Duplicate restoration is after KUB 9.31 III 47. [9] Duplicate restoration follows KUB 9.31 III 49 with additional words *ke-e-el ŠA* KARAŠ, which seem to be omitted here. [10] KUB 9.31 III 50: omits MEŠ. [11] KUB 9.31 III 50: ANŠE.ḪI.A. [12] *ku-it* is superfluous here and not to be found in KUB 9.31 III 50 or 51. [13] Duplicate restoration is after KUB 9.31 III 51. [14] Mistakenly transliterated as UDU.ŠIR-*aš*[ḪI.A] in Dinçol, *Belleten* XLIX/193, 16. [15] KUB 9.31 III 52: adds -*i̯a*. [16] KUB 9.31 III 52: *nu-u̯a-ra-at-*. [17] KUB 9.31 III 53: *ú-e-mi-i̯a-az-*. [18] KUB 9.31 III 53: *i-da-a-lu*. [19] Duplicate restoration follows KUB 9.31 III 54. [20] KUB 9.31 III 55: *ka-ru-ú-u̯a-ri-u-ar*; KUB 41.17 III 5′: [*k*]*a-ru-ú-a-ri-u̯a-ar*. [21] KUB 9.31 III 55, KUB 41.17 III 5′, and KBo 13.212:2′: *ḫu-u-*. [22] Duplicate restoration is after KUB 9.31 III 56, which inserts also ḪI.A. [23] Duplicate restoration follows KUB 9.31 III 56. [24] KUB 41.17 III 6′: [DUG]GAL. [25] KUB 9.31 III 57: [DUG]*ḫu-u-*. [26] Duplicate restoration follows KUB 9.31 III 57; KUB 41.17 III 7′ omits ZABAR. [27] Duplicate restoration follows KUB 9.31 III 57. [28] KUB 9.31 III 58 and KUB 41.17 III 8′: *ta-*. [29] KUB 9.31 III 58 and KUB 41.17 III 8′: *pé-en-ni-*. [30] KBo 13.212:5′ omits -*i̯a*. [31] Duplicate restoration is after KUB 9.31 III 59.

Bo 9713

Description: N/A.

CTH: 832 "*Fragments en langue hittite de nature inconnue*."

Dating and Script: NS.

Remarks: One-sided fragment that is too small to determine.

Measurements: 2.7 × 3.5 × 1.1 cm.

Bibliography: N/A.

Bo 9713

§ 1′ 1′]⸢*x*⸣[

2′]-*x̣*[1)]-*ḫa-aš* ⸢*a-uš-t*⸣[*a*

3′ -*a*]*t*?-*ti* *te-eš-ḫa*-[

4′]- *ḫạ* [

(bottom of the tablet)

Text-critical note: [1)] The broken sign does not look like a "*eš*," thus a restoration [*te-e*]*š-ḫa-aš* is unlikely.

Bo 9715

Description: N/A.

CTH: 831 *"Fragments en langue inconnue ou indéterminée."*

Dating and Script: N/A.

Remarks: One-sided, moderately abraded fragment that has only a few illegible signs. Only recognizable signs are "$TI_8^{MUŠEN}$" (line 1′) and "ŠAḪ" (line 4′).

Measurements: 3.5 × 3.9 × 2.1 cm.

Bibliography: N/A.

Bo 9715

Bo 9716

Description: Festival.

CTH: 635.14.B "*Fragments de fêtes de Zippalanda et du mont Daha.*"

Dating and Script: NS.

Remarks: Bo 9716 is a one-sided fragment whose lines 2′–10′ are duplicate to KUB 41.41 V$^?$ 11′–17′ (CTH 635.14.A; LNS), from where the restorations are taken.

Measurements: 3.6 × 3.9 × 1.1 cm.

Bibliography: Soysal, *Anatolica* 38, 185–86 (transliteration).

Bo 9716

§ 1′ 1′]⸢*x̣*⸣[
2′ [(KÁ.GAL-*aš a*)]*n-da* ⸢*a-ra-an*⸣-[(*zi*)]
3′ [(^{LÚ}A)]LAN.ZU$_9$ *a-ḫa-a ḫal-za-ạ*-[(*i*)]
4′ [(^{LÚ}*ki-i-t*)]*a-aš-ša*[1)] *ḫal-za-ạ-ị* [

---

§ 2′ 5′ [(LUGAL-*uš-kán* K)]Á É MUNUS.LỤGAL ^{URU}*Kạ*-[(*ta-pí*)]
6′ [(*ḫa-an-da-a-i*)]*z-zi* ^{GIŠ}BẠNŠUR-*ụš*[2)]-*š*[(*a*)]
7′ [(*ka-ru-ú a*)]*r-ta* [
8′ [(*na-at-kán I*)]*Š-TU* TÚG[3)] ZA.GÌN *ka*[4)]-*ri-ị*[(*a-an*)]
9′ [(*še-er-ra-aš-ša-an* 1 NINDA.ÉRIN.MEŠ)] ⸤*ki-i*⸥*t-ta-r*[(*i*)]
10′ [(*nu-uš-ša-an še-er tal*)-*l*(*a*$^?$-*i*$^?$ GU)]⸤ŠKI⸥[(N *ŠA* DINGIR-*LIM*)
(broken off)

Text-critical notes: [1)] Dupl. KUB 41.41 V$^?$ 12′ omits -*ša*. [2)] Dupl. KUB 41.41 V$^?$ 14′ omits -*uš*. [3)] Dupl. KUB 41.41 V$^?$ 15′ omits TÚG. [4)] Dupl. KUB 41.41 V$^?$ 15′ adds -*a*-.

Bo 9719

Description: N/A.

CTH: 831 "*Fragments en langue inconnue ou indéterminée.*"

Dating and Script: N/A.

Remarks: Tiny, one-sided fragment with only a few signs. The only recognizable signs are [...]-*x̣-ma* (line 1′) and [...](-)*x̣-ši-ú* (line 2′).

Measurements: 3.3 × 4.1 × 1.5 cm.

Bibliography: N/A.

Bo 9719

Bo 9720

Description: Ritual or festival.

CTH: 470 "*Fragments de rituels*" or 670 "*Fragments divers.*"

Dating and Script: (L)NS.

Remarks: Tiny, one-sided fragment.

Measurements: 3.2 × 2.9 × 1.3 cm.

Bibliography: N/A.

Bo 9720

§ 1′ 1′]⸢*x*(-)*x*⸣[
2′]-*x̣* *d*⸢*a-a*?⸣-[
3′ (.)GE]ŠTIN? *da-ạ*-⸢*ị* ?⸣[

---

§ 2′ 4′]-*x̣* [
5′ I]V *ḫar-za-a*⸤*n-nị*?-*ịš*?⸥[1)][…?]
6′]⸤*x*⸥[
(broken off)

Text-critical note: [1)] Thus, according to the signs not to be read [^{N}]^{INDA}*ḫar-za-z*⸤*u*⸥-. Cf. the only attestation of this noun II *ḫar-za-an-ni-iš* in unpublished Bo 5093 rev.? III 4, for which see Otten, StBoT 15, 27, and Fuscagni, HPMM 6, 97.

Bo 9721

Description: Historical.

CTH: 14.V.C "*Fragments relatifs aux guerres syriennes: nomment Yarim-Lim, Atradu, Ḫammurabi.*"

Dating and Script: OH/NS.

Remarks:: One-sided fragment. Cf. the other fragments from the same text group, which are written likewise in NS: KBo 12.14 (CTH 14.V.A) and Bo 5262 (14.V.B; obv.$^{?}$ 5′–8′ duplicate "A" obv. 4′–6′). The present fragment "C" here could be from the same tablet as "A" or "B"; however, a physical or contextual confirmation is not yet possible.

Measurements: 3.5 × 2.6 × 0.6 cm.

Bibliography: Soysal, *Anatolica* 38, 169–70 (transliteration and commentary).

Bo 9721

§ 1′ 1′] ⌈*ḫa-da-an-da*⌉-[

2′] *ma-am-ma-an* $^{\mathrm{UR⌈U⌉}}$[

3′] *ną-at-ta ḫu-i*[*š*$^{?}$-

4′ (-)*š*]*a*$^{?}$-*aš* ^{URU}*A-na-š*[*a-ap-ri*(-)

5′]-*x̣-ir-lų*$^{?}$-*na-aš*(-)[1)] [

6′ -*l*]*i*$^{?}$-*ma-a*[*n*(-)[2)]

(bottom of the tablet)

Text-critical notes: [1)] The signs in this line cannot be interpreted meaningfully as a Hittite word; however, it is possible that they belong to a non-Hittite geographical name. [2)] A restoration with [^{m}*Ia-ri-im-l*]*i-ma-a*[*n*(-)...], the name of the king of Yamḫad, is conceivable.

Bo 9722

Description: Festival.

CTH: 616.28.T.2 "*AN.TAḪ.ŠUM*^{sar}. *29*^{e} *jour: pour Ea et son groupe.*"

Dating and Script: NS.

Remarks: One-sided fragment whose right-column lines 1′–8′ duplicate KBo 30.69 III 16′–21′ (NS), from where the restorations are taken.

Measurements: 3.7 × 2.2 × 0.4 cm.

Bibliography: Soysal, *Anatolica* 38, 185 (transliteration).

Bo 9722

Left column has only one, illegible sign.

Right column

§ 1′ 1′ ⸢*ti-a*⸣[(*n-zi*) GA(L $^{LÚ.MEŠ}$MUḪALDIM-*ma*)]

2′ GU$_4$-*a*[(*š še-e-ša-an ti-an-zi*)]

3′ *ma-aḫ*-[*ḫa*-(*an-ma-kán*[1]) TU$_7$.ḪI.A)]

4′ *ta-r*[(*u-up-da-ri*) GA(L $^{LÚ.MEŠ}$MUḪALDIM)]

5′ ^{GIŠ}*ḫa-a*[(*p-ša-al-li da-an-zi*)]

6′ *na-aš-t*[(*a* $^{LÚ.MEŠ}$MUḪALDIM)]

7′ *ta-ga-a*[(*n-zi-pu*$^{!}$*-uš*)]

8′ ⸤*ša-ạn-ḫ*⸥[(*a*$^{?}$*-an-zi*)]

(broken off)

Text-critical note: [1] Dupl. KBo 30.69 III 18′: [G]IM-*an-ma-kán*.

Bo 9723

Description: Kizzuwatnan ritual or festival.

CTH: 500 "*Fragments de rituels (ou de fêtes) du Kizzuwatna.*"

Dating and Script: NS.

Remarks: One-sided fragment.

Measurements: 2.6 × 2.5 × 0.9 cm.

Bibliography: N/A.

Bo 9723

§ 1′ 1′]-⸢*x̣*⸣-*zi n*[*u*?(-)

2′]-⸢*a*⸣-*ap-li*(-)*x̣*(-)[1)] [

3′ *k*]*e-el-ti-i̯a* [

4′]-*x̤* ⸢*x*⸣[2)] *ki-iš-ša-*[*an ši-pa-an*(?)-

---

§ 2′ 5′]⸤*x-x x*⸥[

(broken off)

Text-critical notes: [1)] With reservation to be read and restored as [*ša*]-⸢*a*⸣-*ap-li-i̯*[*a*] ? [2)] A "*ki*" sign is erased.

Bo 9724

Description: N/A.

CTH: 832 "*Fragments en langue hittite de nature inconnue*."

Dating and Script: N/A.

Remarks: One-sided, heavily abraded fragment.

Measurements: 4.2 × 2.2 × 1.2 cm.

Bibliography: N/A.

Bo 9724

§ 1′	1′–2′	(traces)
§ 2′	3′	*nụ šị*$^{?}$-[
	4′	(traces)
	5′	*ḫar-tạ*$^{?}$ [
§ 3′	6′	*kụ-i*[*š*$^{?}$-
	7′	*an*-[
	8′	(traces)
	(broken off)	

Bo 9725

Description: Ritual or festival.

CTH: 470 "*Fragments de rituels*" or 670 "*Fragments divers.*"

Dating and Script: NS or LNS.

Remarks: One-sided, moderately abraded fragment.

Measurements: 3.8 × 4.5 × 0.9 cm.

Bibliography: N/A.

Bo 9725

§ 1′ 1′]⌈*x*⌉[

2′] Ẹ́-*ṛị*(?) [

3′](-)*x̣*$^{?}$-*x̣*(-)*x̣*-*šị*$^{?}$-*lị*$^{?}$-*pạ́t*$^{?}$ [

4′] *pạ*$^{?}$-*rạ*-*ạ* *da*-*ạn*-*z*[*i*$^{?}$

5′] *da*-*a*-*ị* [

---

§ 2′ 6′ *A*$^{?}$]-*NA* *x̣*-*x̣*-*x̣*$^{?}$ MUNUS.LUGAL(?) *x̣*(-)[

7′]-*ạn*-*zị*(?) *Ạ*-*NẠ*(?) ^{d}*x̣*(./-)[

8′](-)*x̣*$^{?}$-*x̣*-*x̣* *Ạ*-*NẠ* $^{DỤG?}$⌈*x̣*⌉(.)[

9′ (traces)

(broken off)

Bo 9726

Description: N/A.

CTH: 831 “*Fragments en langue inconnue ou indéterminée*.”

Dating and Script: N/A.

Remarks: Small, one-sided fragment with only a few readable signs.

Measurements: 3.9 × 4.2 × 0.8 cm.

Bibliography: N/A.

Bo 9726

Right column

§ 1′ 1′ *lu*$^{?}$-[

2′ *a*-[

3′ *u̯a*-[

4′ *ši*$^{?}$-[

5′ *ạn*$^{?}$-[

6′ (traces)

(broken off)

Bo 9727

Description: N/A.

CTH: 831 “*Fragments en langue inconnue ou indéterminée.*”

Dating and Script: N/A.

Remarks: Small, one-sided fragment with only a few signs.

Measurements: 4.1 × 4.0 × 0.8 cm.

Bibliography: N/A.

Bo 9727

Left column

§ 1′ 1′ …

---

§ 2′ 2′]-*x̣*

3′–4′ …

5′ -*i̯*]*a*

6′]-⌊*x*-*i̯a*⌋

(broken off)

Right column

(traces only)

Bo 9728

Description: N/A.

CTH: 831 "*Fragments en langue inconnue ou indéterminée*."

Dating and Script: N/A.

Remarks: Small, one-sided fragment with only a few unreadable cuneiform traces.

Measurements: 2.7 × 2.9 × 1.1 cm.

Bibliography: N/A.

Bo 9728

Bo 9729

Description: N/A.

CTH: 831 "*Fragments en langue inconnue ou indéterminée.*"

Dating and Script: N/A.

Remarks: Small, one-sided fragment with only a few signs. Only a sign "[*i̯*]*a*" (line 3′) is certain; perhaps "[G]ÀR" (line 2′).

Measurements: 4.2 × 1.4 × 2.1 cm.

Bibliography: N/A.

Bo 9729

Bo 9730

Description: N/A.

CTH: 831 "*Fragments en langue inconnue ou indéterminée.*"

Dating and Script: N/A.

Remarks: Small, one-sided fragment with only a few unreadable cuneiform traces.

Measurements: 3.1 × 3.3 × 1.0 cm.

Bibliography: N/A.

Bo 9730

Bo 9731

Description: Festival.

CTH: 670 "*Fragments divers.*"

Dating and Script: NS.

Remarks: One-sided fragment from the top portion of a tablet (with upper edge).

Measurements: 1.7 × 3.2 × 1.4 cm.

Bibliography: N/A.

Bo 9731

§ 1 1 LUGAL[?]]-*ị* ŠỤ.ḪI.A-*aš u̯a-a-tar* [

2 *Q*]*A-TỊ*-ḪỊ.Ạ-*ŠỤ a-ar-r*[*i*(-)[1)]

---

§ 2 3 (unreadable sign traces)

(broken off)

Text-critical note: [1)] For similar cult scenes in complete descriptions, cf. KUB 20.85(+) I 7–8: DUMU.MEŠ.É.GAL LUGAL-*i* ŠU.MEŠ-*aš u̯a-a-tar* / *pí-i̯a-an-zi* ŠU.MEŠ-*ŠU a-ar-ri* and KUB 56.45(+) II 16′–17′: DUMU.É.GAL LUGAL-*i* *ME-E QA-TI pé-e-da-i* / LUGAL-*uš* ŠỤ.MEŠ-*ŠỤ a-ar*<-*ri*> etc.

Bo 9732

Description: N/A.

CTH: 831 "*Fragments en langue inconnue ou indéterminée*."

Dating and Script: N/A.

Remarks: One-sided fragment that is too small to classify.

Measurements: 3.1 × 3.2 × 2.7 cm.

Bibliography: N/A.

Bo 9732

§ 1′	1′	](-)*ẋ* LUGAL-*ẋ*(-)[
	2′	](-)*ẋ* LÚ *ẋ*(./-)[
	3′	-*e*]*l-lu*[1)] [
	4′	]-*mị*(-)[
	(broken off)	

Text-critical note: [1)] To be restored as Hittite [*ú-e-e*]*l-lu* ?

Bo 9733

Description: Ritual?.

CTH: 470 "*Fragments de rituels.*"

Dating and Script: N/A.

Remarks: One-sided fragment from the left portion (with edge) of a tablet.

Measurements: 3.3 × 3.4 × 2.2 cm.

Bibliography: N/A.

Bo 9733

§ 1′ 1′ TỤ́G*ši-i*[*k-nu-*[1]

2′ ⌞*nu*? *ki*⌟-[[2]

(illegible signs, then breaks off)

Text-critical notes: [1] The keyword TÚG*ši-i*[*k-nu-*…] makes two reconstructions possible: TÚG*šiknu*(*wa*)*š kattan ēpzi* (a phrase from the Maštigga ritual), or TÚG*šiknun* UGU *pippai* / *pippan* (known from the Pupuwanni ritual). [2] Possibly to be restored as ⌞*nu ki*⌟-[*iš-ša-an me-ma-i* …] like in the Maštigga ritual (KBo 15.1 II 8′–9′, KBo 27.165 + rev. 9′, KBo 39.8 III 25), or as ⌞*nu ki*⌟-[*i* SISKUR-*ŠU* …] like in the Pupuwanni ritual (KBo 15.23 rev. 2′–3′, KUB 7.2 IV 7′–8′, KUB 41.3 + rev. 4′–5′).

Bo 9734

Description: N/A.
CTH: 832 "*Fragments en langue hittite de nature inconnue.*"
Dating and Script: NS$^{?}$.
Remarks: One-sided fragment that is too small to classify.
Measurements: 3.9 × 2.5 × 1.9 cm.
Bibliography: N/A.

Bo 9734

§ 1′ 1′](-)*x̣-x̣ x̣*(-)[
2′ *A*$^{?}$]-*NA* DINGIR.ME[Š
3′]-*aš*$^{?}$-*ma ḫur*-[
4′ -*a*]⸢*d*$^{?}$-*d*⸣*u* [
(broken off)

Bo 9735

Description: N/A.

CTH: 831 "*Fragments en langue inconnue ou indéterminée.*"

Dating and Script: N/A.

Remarks: One-sided fragment that is too small to classify.

Measurements: 3.9 × 4.1 × 1.7 cm.

Bibliography: N/A.

Bo 9735

§ 1′ 1′ -*i*]*n* [
2′]-⌊*š*⌋*a-an*(-)[
3′ (-)*d*]*a*[?]-*a*-*ẋ*(-)[
(broken off)

Bo 9736

Description: N/A.

CTH: 832 "*Fragments en langue hittite de nature inconnue*."

Dating and Script: N/A.

Remarks: One-sided fragment that is too small to classify.

Measurements: 3.1 × 2.5 × 1.0 cm.

Bibliography: N/A.

Bo 9736

§ 1′ 1′ GAL(./-)[

2′ Ẹ̣GIR-[

3′ *i-i̯*[*a-*

(bottom of the tablet)

INDEX OF PROPER NAMES

DIVINE NAMES

^{d}UT[U]	(dat.)	Bo 9625:2′
^{d}UTU-*i*	(dat.)	Bo 9599 + I 11′
^{d}UTU-*aš*	(gen.)	Bo 9698 + :9
[(^{d}UTU)] ([(A)]N-*E*	(voc.)	Bo 9708 + rev. 2′
[^{d}UT(U)] ([(^{URU}Arinn)]a)	(dat.)	Bo 9708 + rev. 5′
^{d}UTU (^{URU}PÚ-*na*)	(voc.)	Bo 9588:7′

Incomplete Divine Names

[^{d}…]-*x-i̯a-an*	(acc.)	Bo 9704:8′
[^{d}…]-*il*	(—)	Bo 9556:4′
[^{d}…-*r*]*i-i̯a*	(dat.$^{?}$)	Bo 9536 + :4′
[^{d}…-*r*]*i*$^{?}$-*i̯a*	(dat.$^{?}$)	Bo 9536 + :5′
[^{d}…]-*ši-i*	(—)	Bo 9556:5′
[^{d}…]-*x-šu-na*	(acc.≠*a*$^{?}$)	Bo 9691:4′
^{d}*Za-l*[*i*$^{?}$-…]	(—)	Bo 9556:4′
[$^{d?}$…-*z*]*i-pa-aš*	(nom.$^{?}$)	Bo 9565:5′
^{d}*x*-[…]	(acc.$^{?}$)	Bo 9691:5′
^{d}*x*(./-)[…]	(dat.$^{?}$)	Bo 9725:7′
⌊^{d}⌋[…]	(—)	Bo 9556:5′
⌊$^{d?}$⌋[…]	(dat.$^{?}$)	Bo 9563:7′

PERSONAL NAMES

^{m}Alakšandu

^{m}*A-l*[(*a-ak-ša-an-du-uš*)]	(nom.)	Bo 9537 + IV 10
^{m}*A-la-ak-ša-a*[*n*]-⌈*du*⌉	(dat.)	Bo 9537 + IV 7

^{m}Anniya

[^{m}*An-n*]*i-i̯*⌈*a*⌉	(dat.$^{?}$)	Bo 9587 + III 1′

^{m}Labarna

[^{m}*La-b*]*a-ar-na*	(gen.)	Bo 9698 + :10

^{m}Muršili

[^{m}*Mu-u*]⌈*r-ši-l*⌉*i*	(nom.)	Bo 9627:1′
^{m}*Mur-ši*-DINGIR-*LIM*	(nom.)	Bo 9653 obv. 1

^{m}Muwa-walwi

^{m}*Mu-ú-a*-UR.MAḪ	(gen.)	Bo 9698 + :10

^{f}Šanḫadu

^{f}*Ša-a*[*n-ḫa-du-uš*]	(nom.)	Bo 9650:5′
[^{f}]*Ša-an-ḫa-du*	(dat.)	Bo 9650:4′

Incomplete Personal Name

^{m}*Pí-ḫa-*⌞*x*⌟ -[…]	(—)	Bo 9682:6′

GEOGRAPHICAL NAMES

^{KUR}Aḫḫiyauwa

^{KUR}*Aḫ-*[*ḫ*]*i-i̯a-u-*[*u̯a*(-)…]	(gen.)	Bo 9698 + :14

^{URU}Anašapri

^{URU}*A-na-š*[*a-ap-ri*(-)…]	(—)	Bo 9721:4′

^{URU}Ankuwa

[^{UR}]^{U}*An-ku-*⌜*u̯*⌝*a*	(gen.)	Bo 9702:2′
[^{UR}]^{U}*An-ku-u̯a-a*[*š*]	(gen.)	Bo 9663:5′

^{URU}Apzuwa

[^{UR}]^{U}*Ap*(?)*-zu-u-i-*	(dat.-loc.)	Bo 9582:6′

^{URU}Arinna

[(^{URU}*A-ri-in-n*)]*a*	(gen.)	Bo 9708 + rev. 5′
		see also under **^{URU}PÚ-na**

^{URU}Arzauwa

^{URU}*Ar-za-u-u̯a*	(gen.)	Bo 9615 + I 1

^{URU}Ḫayaša

^{URU}*Ḫa-i̯a-ša*	(loc.)	Bo 9587 + III 6′

^{URU}Ḫalenzuwa

^{URU}*Ḫa-l*⌜*e*⌝*-*⌞*e*⌟*n-zu-u̯a*	(gen.)	Bo 9536 + :7′
$^{\mathrm{UR⌜U⌝}}$[*Ḫ*]*a-le-en-zu-*[*u̯a*]	(gen.$^{?}$)	Bo 9536 + :9′

KUR ^{URU}Ḫatti

KUR ^{URU}*Ḫa-at-ti*	(acc.)	Bo 9614 left col. 3
KUR ^{URU}*Ḫa-at-ti*	(abl.)	Bo 9537 + IV 10
KUR ^{URU}*Ḫa-at-ti*	(gen.)	Bo 9569 + IV 28
[KUR ^{UR}]^{U}*Ḫa-at-ti*	(gen.)	Bo 9637 + IV 31
[KUR ^{URU}*Ḫ*]*a-at-ti*	(gen.)	Bo 9627:2′
		see also under **KUR ^{URU}PA-ti**

^{URU}Ḫattuša

^{URU}*Ḫa-at-tu-š[a-aš]*	(nom.)	Bo 9537 + IV 11
		see also under **^{URU}KÙ.BABBAR**

^{URU}Ḫimmuwa

[^{URU}*Ḫ*]*i-im-mu-u̯a*	(gen.)	Bo 9579:2′

^{URU}Ištetena

^{URU}*Iš-te-te-na-*	(gen.)	Bo 9587 + III 8′

^{URU}Katapa

^{URU}*Ka-*[(*ta-pí*)]	(loc.)	Bo 9716:5′

^{URU}Kazzapa

[^{URU}*Ka*$^{?}$]*-az-za-p*[*a*(-)…]	(—)	Bo 9652:5′

^{URU}Nerik(a)

^{URU}*Ne-ri-ik*	(gen.$^{?}$)	Bo 9536 + :9′
^{URU}*N*⸢*e*⸣-[*ri*$^{?}$*-ik*$^{?}$]	(gen.)	Bo 9536 + :6′
[^{URU}*N*]*e-ri- ik*	(gen.)	Bo 9536 + :6′
^{URU}*N*[*e-ri-ik-ka*$_{4}$]	(gen.)	Bo 9598 II$^{?}$ 2′

^{URU}Šamuḫa

[^{UR}]^{U}*Ša-m*[*u-ḫa-aš*]	(gen.)	Bo 9663:6′

(KUR) ^{URU}Dankuwa

^{URU}*Da-an-ku-u̯a*	(loc.)	Bo 9587 + III 4′
KUR ^{URU}*Da-an-ku-u̯*[*a*]	(loc.)	Bo 9587 + III 9′

^{URU}Zipalanda

[^{UR}]^{U}*Zi-p*⸤*a*⸥*-l*⸤*a-a*⸥*n-da*	(gen.$^{?}$)	Bo 9626:7′
[^{U}]^{RU}*Zi-pa-la-an-da*(-)[…]	(—)	Bo 9626:4′

^{URU}KÙ.BABBAR

^{URU}KÙ.BABBAR$^{?}$(-)*x*$^{?}$(-)[…]	(—)	Bo 9699:6″
		see also under **^{URU}Ḫattuša**

KUR ^{URU}PA-ti

[KUR ^{U}]^{RU}PA-*ti*	(—)	Bo 9626:5′
		see also under **KUR ^{URU}Ḫatti**

^{URU}PÚ-na

^{URU}PÚ-*na*	(gen.)	Bo 9588:7′
^{URU}PÚ-*na*	(dat.)	Bo 9698 + :9
		see also under **^{URU}Arinna**

Incomplete Geographical Name

MOUNTAIN NAMES

$^{\text{ḪUR.SAG}}$Našalma

Incomplete Mountain Names

SELECT LEXICAL ENTRIES FROM Bo 9536 – Bo 9736

This section is dedicated to the selected lexemes and does not claim to be a complete word list of the fragments Bo 9536–Bo 9736. It should mainly focus on *hapax legomena*, rare forms and spellings, and those words that are now in their corrected and completed forms as one can reveal from the recent (direct) joins and duplicates. Although their number is not in plenty, these occurrences will be useful for future lexical studies. For reasons of space, the occurrences are cited with Bo-numbers only, and line numberings are always in accordance with those given in the transliteration section.

SYLLABIC WORDS

an-ni-iš-kán-zi	Bo 9580:5′ **iter. pres. pl. 3** ➔ *aniya-* “to do, perform”
ạ-pu-u-u[*š*]	Bo 9708 + rev. 4′ **pl. acc. com.** ➔ *apa-* “that one”
a-ar-ti	Bo 9673 + II 82 **pres. sg. 2** ➔ *ar-* “to arrive at”
[^{LÚ}]*ạ-ra-aš*	Bo 9639:7′ **sg. nom. com.** ➔ ^{LÚ}*ara-* “friend, colleague”
[^{LÚ}]*ạ-ra-aš-š*(*a*)	Bo 9639:8′ **sg. nom. com.** ➔ ^{LÚ}*ara-* “friend, colleague”
ar-ma-a-[*la-aš*]	Bo 9628 + II 25′ **sg. nom. com.** ➔ *armala-* “sick, ill”
ạ-ru-e-eš-ki-u̯-[*u̯a*$^{?}$*-an*]	Bo 9585:5′ **sup.** ➔ *aruwai-* “to bow”
^{GIŠ}*ḫa-aḫ*$^{!}$*-ri*	Bo 9695 rt. col. 2′ **sg. dat.-loc. com.** ➔ ^{GIŠ}*ḫaḫra-* “rake$^{?}$”

ḫal-k⌊u-ú-i⌋-eš-šar(-ra)
Bo 9605 + I$^{?}$ 7′ (also I$^{?}$ 4′ ?)
sg. nom.-acc. neut.
➔ *ḫalkueššar* “(cultic) supplies”

ḫạ-lu-gạ-aš
Bo 9650:3′
sg. nom. com.
➔ *ḫaluga-* “message”

ḫal-zi-iḫ-ḫị
Bo 9577:2′
pres. sg. 1
➔ *ḫalziya-* “to call”

ḫal-z[i-i̯]a-u-e-ni
Bo 9599 + I 12′
pres. pl. 1
➔ *ḫalziya-* “to call”

ḫar-za-a⌊n-nị$^{?}$-ịš$^{?}$⌋
Bo 9720:5′
sg. nom. com.$^{?}$
➔ *ḫarzanni-* (noun, unkn. mng.)

ḫa-aš-pé-el-lạ
Bo 9605 + I$^{?}$ 6′
➔ *ḫašpel(a)-* (noun, unkn. mng.)

[ḫ]a$^{?}$-tu-ki
Bo 9597:3″
sg. dat.-loc.$^{?}$
➔ *ḫatuka-* “terrifying”

ḫu-u-el-pí (modifying GA “milk”)
Bo 9605 + I$^{?}$ 5′
sg. nom.-acc. neut.
➔ *ḫuelpi-* “tender, fresh”

ḫu-u-e-ša-u̯a-az
Bo 9702:3′
sg. abl.
➔ *ḫuešu-* “raw (meat)”

[$^{UZU?}$*ḫu-uḫ-ḫ*]*ụ-ur-ti-i*⸢*š*⸣*-x̣*$^{?}$(-)
Bo 9548:2′
sg. nom. com.
➔ $^{(UZU)}$*ḫuḫḫurti-* “throat”

ị-i̯a-an-ni-i̯a-zị
Bo 9677:7′
pres. sg. 3
➔ *iyanniya-* “to go, march”

^{UDU}*i-i̯a-an-t⌊a⌋-[aš$^{?}$]*
Bo 9689 u. e. 1
sg. gen.$^{?}$ com.
➔ ^{UDU}*iyant-* “sheep”

[i]n-na-ra-u-a⌊n⌋-[ni]

Bo 9614 lt. col. 4

sg. dat.-loc. neut.

➔ *innarawatar-* "strength"

[GIŠ? in-t]a-lu-uz-z[i(-)…]

Bo 9597:6″

➔ GIŠ*intaluzzi-* "shovel?"

⌊i⌋š-ḫa-aḫ-ru-[u̯]a-aš

Bo 9628 + II 21′

gen. neut.

➔ *išḫaḫru-* "tear(s)"

⌊iš?⌋-ḫa-aš-šar-u-e-eš-du

Bo 9679 + V 2

imp. sg. 3

➔ *išḫaššarweš-* "to act in a lordly manner"

[iš?-ḫ]u-u-u̯a-aš

Bo 9570:5′

pret. sg. 3

➔ *išḫuwai-* "to pour, scatter"

iš-ta-ma-aš-ti

Bo 9673 + II 80

pres. sg. 2

➔ *ištamaš-* "to hear"

ka-⌊a-š⌋[a(-)…]

Bo 9630:4′

➔ *kāša* "behold"

kat+t[a-an]

Bo 9595:3′

➔ *kattan* "under"

kat+ti(-iš-mi)

Bo 9595:2′

dat.-loc.

➔ *katta* "with"

ki-an-ta-ri

Bo 9615 + I 3′

mid. pres. pl. 3

➔ *ki-* "to lie, be placed"

É*kip-pa-⌈a⌉[n]*

Bo 9575:3′

sg. acc. com.

➔ É*kippa-* (a building or structure)

⌊ki-i-ša⌋-ạt

Bo 9628 + II 22′

pret. sg. 3

➔ *kiš-* "to become"

^{KUŠ}*kur-šu-uš*	Bo 9580:7′ **pl. acc. com.** ➔ ^{KUŠ}*kurša-* “hunting bag$^{?}$”
kụ-ru-ta-a-u-u̯a-an-za	Bo 9541:2′ **sg. nom. com.** ➔ *kurutawant-* “clothed with a *k*.”
li-la-aš(-)	Bo 9550:4′ **sg. nom.** or **gen. com.** ➔ *lila-* “conciliation”
[*l*]*u-ú-li-aš*	Bo 9669:3′ **sg. gen. com.** ➔ *luli-* “pond; spring”
ma-la-an-z[*i*]	Bo 9598 II$^{?}$/III$^{?}$ 5′ **pres. pl. 3** ➔ *malla/i-* “to mill, grind”
ma-am-ma-an	Bo 9721:2′ ➔ *mān+man* “even if …”
⌊^{NINDA}*ma-ri*⌋*-i-*⌊*e-eš*⌋	Bo 9612 I$^{?}$ 2′ ➔ ^{NINDA}*mari-* “bread stick$^{?}$”
<*me-*>*ma-i*	Bo 9647 + KUB 35.13:10′ **pres. sg. 3** ➔ *mema-* “to speak”
me-mi-i̯a-an-n[*i*]	Bo 9537 + IV 12 **sg. dat.-loc. neut.** ➔ *memiya*(*n*)*-* “word”
⌊*me-e*⌋*-ni-aš* (with preceding [MU-*t*]⌊*i*$^{?}$⌋)	Bo 9628 + II 25′ **sg. gen. com.** ➔ *mēni-* “course”
[*n*]*e-i̯ạ-ạt-tạ-ạt*$^{?}$	Bo 9698 +:13 **mid. pret. sg. 3** ➔ *neya-* “to turn oneself”
pa-an-ku-ni-i[*t*]	Bo 9559:5′ **sg. inst. neut.** ➔ *pankur-* “clan$^{?}$”

pár-ḫu-i-na-aš	Bo 9612 I$^{?}$ 4′ **sg. nom. com.** ➔ *parḫuina-* (a kind of grain)
p̣ạ́r$^{?}$-ki-i̯a-an-za	Bo 9673 + II 77 **part. sg. nom. com.** ➔ *parkiya-* “to lift / take away”
pé-e-di	Bo 9628 + II 24′ **sg. dat.-loc. neut.** ➔ *peda-* “place”
⸢*pí-d*⸣*ạ-ạn-zi* (with preceding *ar-ḫa*)	Bo 9712 + obv.25 **pres. pl. 3** ➔ *peda-* “to carry”
pé-e-dạ-aš (with preceding *ka*[*t-t*]*a-an-ta*)	Bo 9587 + III 6′ **pret. sg. 3** ➔ *peda-* “to carry”
p̣ít-tụ-li-iš-ki-mi	Bo 9628 + II 23′ **iter. pres. sg. 1** ➔ *pittuliya-* “to worry”
pu-u-ri-i[*n*]	Bo 9602 (+$^{?}$) coloph. 2′ **sg. acc. com.** ➔ *puri-* “lip”
pu-u-tal-l[*i-…*]	Bo 9640:5′ ➔ *putalliya-* “to tie on / together”
𒑱$^{?}$*ša-kán-ta-at-tar*(-)	Bo 9576:3′ **sg.$^{?}$ nom.-acc. neut.** ➔ *šakantattar* “appliqué$^{?}$”
[*še*]*-ḫi-li-iš-ki-aš*	Bo 9577:4′ **sg. gen.$^{?}$ com.** ➔ *šeḫiliški-* “purification ritual / offering”
še-pí-tàš	Bo 9550:5′ **sg. gen. neut.** ➔ *šepit* (a kind of grain)
[*š*]*u$^{?}$-un-na-an-tẹ-*[*eš*]	Bo 9543:3′ **part. pl. nom. com.** ➔ *šunna-* “to fill”

da-a-ú

Bo 9712 + obv.32
imp. sg. 3
➔ *da-* “to take”

[$^{\text{LÚ.MEŠ}}$*t*]*a*$^{?}$*-ḫi-i̯a-le-e*[*š*(-)…]

Bo 9704:7′
pl. nom. com.
➔ ^{LÚ}*taḫiyali-* “barber$^{?}$”

[$^{\text{LÚ.MEŠ}}$*ta*$^{?}$]-⌊*ḫi-i̯*⌋*a-le-e*[*š*(-)…]

Bo 9704:9′
pl. nom. com.
➔ ^{LÚ}*taḫiyali-* “barber$^{?}$”

$^{\text{EZEN}_4}$*da-ḫi-i̯a-aš*

Bo 9605 + Bo 3396 + I$^{?}$ 3′
sg. gen. com.
➔ $^{\text{EZEN}_4}$*daḫiya-* (a festival)

da-a-i⌊*š-ta-an*⌋(-)

Bo 9654:2′
part. sg.$^{?}$ nom.-acc. neut.
➔ *daištai-* “to load”

da-ạ-lu-ga-aš

Bo 9632 rev. III$^{?}$ 4
sg. nom. com.
➔ *daluga-* “long”

[*ta-ma-a*]*t-ta*

Bo 9628 + II 24′
sg. dat. neut.
➔ *tamai-* “to another …”

tar-ma-a-⌈*iz*⌋*-zi* (with preceding *kat-ta*)

Bo 9647 +:9′
pres. sg. 3
➔ *tarmai-* “to nail down”

tar-na-lu-li

Bo 9637 + IV 31
sg. dat.-loc.
➔ *tarnaluli* (a sacred location)

^{É}*tar-nu-u-ẹ-e*[*š*$^{?}$(-)…]

Bo 9658:1′
pl. nom. com.
➔ ^{É}*tarnu-* “bath house”

^{GIŠ}*tar-za-u*(?)*-an*

Bo 9677:8′
adj. sg. nom.-acc. neut.
➔ ^{GIŠ}*tarzuwan* “*tarzu*-furnished”

[d]a$^{?}$-a-šụ-ẹš	Bo 9632 rev. III$^{?}$ 2 **pl. nom. com.** ➔ *daššu-* “strong, heavy”
tu-e-da-za	Bo 9626:6′ **abl.** ➔ *zik* “you”
^{LÚ}*tu-uḫ-kán-ti-i̯[a$^{?}$-…]*	Bo 9588:3′ **sg. dat.** or **gen. com.** ➔ ^{LÚ}*tuḫkanti-* “crown prince”
up-pa-ụ́$^{?}$	Bo 9562:4′ **imp. sg. 3** ➔ *uppa-* “to send here”
uš-ká[n-du(?)]	Bo 9537 + IV 14 **imp. pl. 3** ➔ *ušk-* “to watch”
ú-u̯a-te-nu-un	Bo 9698 +:9 **pret. sg. 1** ➔ *uwate-* “to bring here”
ụ́-e-ek-ti	Bo 9584:4′ **pres. sg. 2** ➔ *wek-* “to wish, desire”
za-ap-pí-iš-ki-ị[z-zi]	Bo 9628 + II 24′ **iter. pres. sg. 3** ➔ *zappiya-* “to drip away”
[z]i-ig-g(a-mu-uš-ša-an)	Bo 9673 + II 81 **nom.** ➔ *zik* “you”
[z]ị$^{?}$-nạ$^{?}$-ịl(-)	Bo 9543:4′ **sg. nom.-acc. neut.** ➔ *zinail* “chick pea$^{?}$”
zi-nịr(-)	Bo 9555:4′ ➔ *zinir* “music$^{?}$”

LOGOGRAMS AND AKKADOGRAMS

BURU$_{14}$	Bo 9689 obv. 4 ➔ BURU$_{14}$ "harvest(time)"
[^{GIŠ}DÌ]M	Bo 9566 lt. col. 1′, 2′ ➔ ^{GIŠ}DÌM "pillar$^{?}$"
DÙ-*an-zi*	Bo 9536 +:8′, 10′ **pres. pl. 3** ➔ DÙ / *iya-* "to do"
DÙ-*ạt*	Bo 9632 obv. II$^{?}$ 4′ **pret. sg. 3** ➔ DÙ / *iya-* "to do"
ÉRIN.ME.EŠ	Bo 9595:3′ **pl. acc. com.** ➔ ÉRIN "soldier"
GIŠ.RÍN ZI.BA.N[A]	Bo 9557 + I 16 ➔ GIŠ.RÍN ZI.BA.NA "scales"
KẠR-*at*$^{?}$	Bo 9632 obv. II$^{?}$ 6′ **pret. sg. 3** ➔ KAR / *wemiya-* "to find"
KUŠ.BABBAR	Bo 9680 rev.$^{?}$ 4′ ➔ KUŠ.BABBAR "white hide"
LIBIR-*RU*	Bo 9568:3′ **sg. nom.** or **acc.** ➔ LIBIR "old"
[L]IBIR$^{?}$-*RI*	Bo 9590:3′ **sg.** / **pl. dat.** or **gen.** ➔ LIBIR "old"
SIG.KÙŠ	Bo 9541:3′ ➔ SIG.KÙŠ "small cubit"
ŠỤ.ḪI.A-*aš*	Bo 9731:1 **pl. gen.** ➔ ŠU "hand"

[U]Ḫ$_7$-*an-za*	Bo 9615 + I 1′
	part. sg. nom. com.
	➔ UḪ$_7$-*ant-* / *alwanzaḫḫant-* "bewitched"
ZALAG.GA.A(?)	Bo 9645:8′
	➔ ZALAG.GA "bright, illuminated"
[L]Ú?*ṬE*$_4$-*ME*	Bo 9580:6′
	➔ LÚ*ṬEMU* "messenger"

LEXICAL CITATIONS

In the following are listed the words from the treated Bo-texts and related lexical entries from the Hittite lexicon. There are no detailed discussions, but brief remarks which are necessary for some lexical topics.

HITTITE

(SEMI-)LOGOGRAPHIC WORDS AND AKKADOGRAMS

HATTIAN

HURRIAN

LUWIAN

CITATIONS FROM OTHER BOĞAZKÖY TEXTS

The citations from other Boğazköy texts that concern lexical and textual details are listed here under the related Bo- and "text-critical notes" numbers. The duplicate text entries as part of *textual apparatus* are not included.

Bo 3123 IV 6′–8′	Bo 9543 n. 2
Bo 3315 + obv. 8′	Bo 9598 n. 1
Bo 3315 + obv. 9′	Bo 9598 n. 2
Bo 5093 rev.$^{?}$ III 4	Bo 9720 n. 1
ABoT 17 + III 6′	Bo 9607 n. 1
FHG 2 + KUB 33.53 III 18′	Bo 9570 n. 1
FHG 2 + KUB 33.53 III 20′, 24′	Bo 9570 n. 2
IBoT 2.93 obv. 14′–16′	Bo 9543 n. 2
IBoT 3.11:1′, 4′–5′	Bo 9536 + n. 1
IBoT 4.22 obv. 1′	Bo 9612 n. 3
IBoT 4.22 obv. 3′–5′	Bo 9612 n. 2
IBoT 4.27 obv. 1–3	Bo 9665 (+$^{?}$) n. 1 and n. 2
IBoT 4.137 II 3′	Bo 9566 n. 1
KBo 2.4 III 12′–13′	Bo 9702 n. 1
KBo 2.7 obv. 16′	Bo 9568 n. 2
KBo 2.9 + I 21′	Bo 9636 n. 1
KBo 2.13 obv. 16	Bo 9702 n. 5
KBo 2.13 obv. 17	Bo 9702 nn. 3–4
KBo 4.10+ rev. 1	Bo 9663 n. 1 and n. 3
KBo 4.10+ rev. 2	Bo 9663 n. 2
KBo 8.35 II 24′	Bo 9595 n. 1
KBo 8.35 II 30′–31′	Bo 9595 n. 4
KBo 8.117 II 7′	Bo 9706 n. 2
KBo 8.117 II 8′	Bo 9706 n. 1
KBo 11.41 I 8′–10′	Bo 9543 n. 2
KBo 12.111:1′–5′	Bo 9597 n. 1
KBo 13.145 rev.$^{?}$ 9′	Bo 9680 n. 3
KBo 14.84 IV 5′–7′	Bo 9710 n. 3
KBo 15.1 II 8′–9′	Bo 9733 n. 2
KBo 15.23 rev. 2′–3′	Bo 9733 n. 2
KBo 16.29(+) I$^{?}$ 12′–20′	Bo 9595 n. 4
KBo 16.49+ I 11′–12′	Bo 9669 n. 1
KBo 17.105+ III 6–9	Bo 9597 n. 1

CONCORDANCE OF THE CTH-NUMBERS OF Bo 9536 – Bo 9736 ACCORDING TO "CHDS 2" AND "KONKORDANZ"

Bo	*CHDS 2*	*Konkordanz (as of 31.12.2014)*
9536 +	530 or 670	530
9537 +	76.B	76.B
9538	670	832
9539	670	832
9541	522	832
9542	787	832
9543	677?	832
9544	470	832
9545	832	832
9547	832	832
9548	470 or 670	832
9549	832	832
9550	530	832
9553	670	832
9554	470 or 670	832
9555	670	832
9556	670	832
9557 +	780.II.1.T.A	780.II.1.T.A
9559	212 or 275	832
9560	427	832
9561	68.N	68.N
9562	832	832
9563	670	832
9564	831	832
9565	832	832
9566	670	832
9567	832	832
9568	530	832
9569 +	483.II.A	483.II.A
9570	832	832
9571 +	483.II.A	483.II.A
9572	832	832
9573	670	832
9574	470 or 670	832
9575	401	832
9576	582	832

Bo	*CHDS 2*	*Konkordanz (as of 31.12.2014)*
9577	590	832
9578	832	832
9579	670	832
9580	530 or 670	832
9581	470 or 670	832
9582	343.7	343.7
9583	250 or 530	832
9584	470	832
9585	832	832
9586	832	832
9587 +	61.II.4	61.II.4
9588	385	832
9589	530	832
9590	470 or 670	832
9591	832	832
9593	770	832
9594	470 or 670	832
9595	139	139.2
9596	832	832
9597	832	832
9598	678.3.F	832
9599 +	395	395
9601	832	832
9602 (+$^{?}$)	470 or 670	832
9603	832	832
9604	670	832
9605 +	574.21	574.21
9606	470 or 670	832
9607	832	832
9608	832	832
9609	832	832
9610	470 or 670	832
9611	470 or 670	832
9612	409	832
9614	324.3.F	324.3.F
9615 +	402.G	402.G
9616	832	832
9617	470 or 670	832
9619	770	832
9620	832	832
9621	831	832
9623	832	832
9625	670	832
9626	389	832
9627	832	832

Bo	*CHDS 2*	*Konkordanz (as of 31.12.2014)*
9628 +	374.2.A	374.2.A
9630	394.I	410
9631	832	832
9632	736.9	736.9
9634	500	832
9635	832	832
9636	832	832
9637 +	483.II.A	483.II.A
9638	470 or 670	832
9639	670	832
9640	470	832
9641	832	832
9642	832	832
9643	832	832
9644	670	832
9645	470	832
9646	470 or 670	832
9647 +	763	763
9648	832	832
9650	341.III.22	832
9651	470 or 670	832
9652	215	832
9653	832	832
9654	470 or 670	832
9657	470 or 670	832
9658	832	832
9659 +	374.2.A	374.2.A
9660	470	832
9661	470	832
9662	645.8	645.8
9663	212 or 213	832
9664	832	832
9665 (+$^{?}$)	490.1.A.6	490.1.A.6
9667	670	832
9668	832	832
9669	670	832
9670	832	832
9671	669	832
9673 +	42.A	42.A
9674	470, 530 or 670	832
9675	832	832
9677	470	832
9678	831	832
9679 +	669.4.A	669.4.A
9680	470 or 670	832

Bo	*CHDS 2*	*Konkordanz (as of 31.12.2014)*
9681	250, 470, or 670	832
9682	590	832
9683	832	832
9686	831	832
9688	670	832
9689	210	832
9691	670	832
9692	470 or 670	832
9693	470 or 670	832
9695	470 or 670	832
9696	470 or 670	832
9697	670	832
9698 +	211.4	211.4
9699	215	832
9700	275	832
9701	470 or 670	832
9702	530 or 670	832
9704	670	832
9705	470 or 590	832
9706	470 or 670	832
9708 +	419.G	419.G
9710	470 or 670	832
9711	832	832
9712 +	394.C	394.C
9713	832	832
9715	831	832
9716	635.14.B	635.14.B
9719	831	832
9720	470 or 670	832
9721	14.V.C	14.V.C
9722	616.28.T.2	616.Tg28.2
9723	500	832
9724	832	832
9725	470 or 670	832
9726	831	832
9727	831	832
9728	831	832
9729	831	832
9730	831	832
9731	670	832
9732	831	832
9733	470	832
9734	832	832
9735	831	832
9736	832	832